I0434987

HONG KONG: A BROKEN PROMISE?

HEARING

BEFORE THE

SUBCOMMITTEE ON ASIA AND THE PACIFIC

OF THE

COMMITTEE ON FOREIGN AFFAIRS
HOUSE OF REPRESENTATIVES

ONE HUNDRED THIRTEENTH CONGRESS

SECOND SESSION

DECEMBER 2, 2014

Serial No. 113–226

Printed for the use of the Committee on Foreign Affairs

Available via the World Wide Web: http://www.foreignaffairs.house.gov/ or
http://www.gpo.gov/fdsys/

U.S. GOVERNMENT PRINTING OFFICE

91–662PDF WASHINGTON : 2014

For sale by the Superintendent of Documents, U.S. Government Printing Office
Internet: bookstore.gpo.gov Phone: toll free (866) 512–1800; DC area (202) 512–1800
Fax: (202) 512–2104 Mail: Stop IDCC, Washington, DC 20402–0001

COMMITTEE ON FOREIGN AFFAIRS

EDWARD R. ROYCE, California, *Chairman*

CHRISTOPHER H. SMITH, New Jersey
ILEANA ROS-LEHTINEN, Florida
DANA ROHRABACHER, California
STEVE CHABOT, Ohio
JOE WILSON, South Carolina
MICHAEL T. McCAUL, Texas
TED POE, Texas
MATT SALMON, Arizona
TOM MARINO, Pennsylvania
JEFF DUNCAN, South Carolina
ADAM KINZINGER, Illinois
MO BROOKS, Alabama
TOM COTTON, Arkansas
PAUL COOK, California
GEORGE HOLDING, North Carolina
RANDY K. WEBER SR., Texas
SCOTT PERRY, Pennsylvania
STEVE STOCKMAN, Texas
RON DeSANTIS, Florida
DOUG COLLINS, Georgia
MARK MEADOWS, North Carolina
TED S. YOHO, Florida
SEAN DUFFY, Wisconsin
CURT CLAWSON, Florida

ELIOT L. ENGEL, New York
ENI F.H. FALEOMAVAEGA, American
  Samoa
BRAD SHERMAN, California
GREGORY W. MEEKS, New York
ALBIO SIRES, New Jersey
GERALD E. CONNOLLY, Virginia
THEODORE E. DEUTCH, Florida
BRIAN HIGGINS, New York
KAREN BASS, California
WILLIAM KEATING, Massachusetts
DAVID CICILLINE, Rhode Island
ALAN GRAYSON, Florida
JUAN VARGAS, California
BRADLEY S. SCHNEIDER, Illinois
JOSEPH P. KENNEDY III, Massachusetts
AMI BERA, California
ALAN S. LOWENTHAL, California
GRACE MENG, New York
LOIS FRANKEL, Florida
TULSI GABBARD, Hawaii
JOAQUIN CASTRO, Texas

AMY PORTER, *Chief of Staff*   THOMAS SHEEHY, *Staff Director*
JASON STEINBAUM, *Democratic Staff Director*

————

SUBCOMMITTEE ON ASIA AND THE PACIFIC

STEVE CHABOT, Ohio, *Chairman*

DANA ROHRABACHER, California
MATT SALMON, Arizona
MO BROOKS, Alabama
GEORGE HOLDING, North Carolina
SCOTT PERRY, Pennsylvania
DOUG COLLINS, Georgia
CURT CLAWSON, Florida

ENI F.H. FALEOMAVAEGA, American
  Samoa
AMI BERA, California
TULSI GABBARD, Hawaii
BRAD SHERMAN, California
GERALD E. CONNOLLY, Virginia
WILLIAM KEATING, Massachusetts

(II)

CONTENTS

HONG KONG: A BROKEN PROMISE?

TUESDAY, DECEMBER 2, 2014

HOUSE OF REPRESENTATIVES,
SUBCOMMITTEE ON ASIA AND THE PACIFIC,
COMMITTEE ON FOREIGN AFFAIRS,
Washington, DC.

The subcommittee met, pursuant to notice, at 2:02 p.m., in room 2172, Rayburn House Office Building, Hon. Steve Chabot (chairman of the subcommittee) presiding.

Mr. CHABOT. Good afternoon. The committee will come to order. And before we begin this afternoon, I would like to take a moment just to say a few words about my good friend, the ranking member, Eni Faleomavaega. As this is likely to be the last hearing, we think, of the Asia-Pacific Subcommittee in this Congress, this will be the last time that I will have the honor to sit on this dais next to my good friend Eni, from American Samoa. And I can tell you I am going to miss that experience, opportunity, and real honor it has been. He is truly one of the class acts of the United States Congress.

I have served on this committee for 18 years now. And that pales in comparison, I think, to how long Eni has been on the committee. But I have gotten to know him quite well over the years and have gotten to know him even better after 2001. During that year, Eni and I both served as the representatives from the Congress to the U.N. We went to the U.N. headquarters a number of times and worked on various issues right after that year. It was right after September 11, so it was a very active time when it comes to international affairs.

And our friendship has grown over the years as we have traveled on a number of occasions to different parts of the world, mainly in Asia. This last year, we were in South Korea, Japan, and Taiwan, where we met with heads of state, including in a prison with former President Chen Shui-bian of Taiwan. I think we both agree he has been in prison long enough, and for whatever he did he certainly served a penalty for that. We certainly think that justice has been served, and he should get humanitarian parole. I didn't want to get sidetracked too much on that, but I feel very strongly about that particular issue, and I know Eni does as well.

Because world leaders have dealt with him before, they have seen him in action, and they know the humanness of this person, you find out during these trips the high regard that Eni is held in the eyes of world leaders all over this globe. He really does care and he cares about the people of American Samoa. But he cares about American Samoa just as much as he cares about the whole world because he is truly a man of the world and has made this world a better place.

As I think most people know, he served our country honorably, wearing the uniform of our country in Vietnam. A lot of us talk about these things, but Eni has experienced them firsthand. We don't always agree on everything. I am a little bit on the right, and he is a little bit on the left. Probably people would say I am way out on the right and he is maybe a little further to the left than a little out on the left. But that being the fact, this is a time when bipartisanship really has worked in many ways.

And so I want to thank him for his friendship, his leadership on this committee, and his leadership in Congress. He will truly be missed and truly not forgotten. He is one of the few Members that has a photo of himself on the wall with Elvis Presley, and as I think somebody mentioned, was in a movie with Elvis Presley. I mean, that is pretty impressive stuff.

But, again, in all seriousness, we appreciate your service to our country and to this committee, Eni. And I also want to say that in his absence when he had health issues, Ami Bera stepped up and really did a very commendable job coheading the committee with me. That is really what happens around here, is we work together on these things in the Foreign Affairs Committee.

Before I get into my opening statement, I would welcome any other members that might, should the spirit move them, like to say something.

Mr. Bera.

Mr. BERA. I would just echo the statements. As a freshman Member of Congress, Eni has been a great role model, and helped me navigate the Foreign Affairs Committee.

And you are not disappearing. You will still be around as a resource, certainly, to this freshman Member of Congress, and soon to be sophomore Member. So thank you for everything you have done, and I do look forward to continuing to work with you.

Mr. CHABOT. Would the gentleman from Pennsylvania like to say something.

Mr. PERRY. Sure. Also appreciate and want to echo the chairman's remarks. We have not served together long and only on few occasions in this subcommittee, mostly in the course of the full committee. But I have appreciated your perspective. And whether we agree or disagree, there is no doubt that you are a strong advocate for your constituency at home, and that is what they expect. And so I applaud you for standing firm for what you believe and for your constituents. We hope that we can all serve with the same measure. So I wish you God's speed.

Mr. CHABOT. Thank you.

The gentleman from California, who has served for quite some time not only with myself, but with the gentleman from American Samoa.

Mr. SHERMAN. Echo your comments, Mr. Chairman. I have been on the full committee with Eni for 18 years. I have learned more about American Samoa than I ever thought possible and more about the issues of the Pacific and of Asia. And I would say he is going to be missed, but hopefully he will still be here. That will be the one thing that prevents him from being missed. So, we look forward to gaining Mr. Faleomavaega's counsel and input on foreign policy as the years go forward.

Mr. CHABOT. Thank you very much.

And if the gentleman would like to say anything, he is welcome to now or he can wait till the opening statement.

Okay. Thank you very much. I will now proceed with my statement.

For 2 months, the people of Hong Kong have come together to protest Beijing's decision to deny the city's 7.2 million people the right to directly elect their Chief Executive, putting the future of democracy in Hong Kong at great risk. The demise of the ''One Country, Two System'' framework of governance is a stark reminder that Beijing's promises can be revoked at the drop of a hat.

What we see in Hong Kong today, however, is not an isolated event. It is the latest chapter in the story of an increasingly aggressive China that began 2 years ago when President Xi Jinping assumed power. Under Xi's leadership, a new brand of Chinese nationalism has emerged, and it is one where China takes the center stage in international affairs by asserting its hegemony in the region and directly challenging the United States.

Domestically, the stifling of dissent has risen to new levels extending even to the economic front where the government's antimonopoly laws are targeting American companies. Beijing is also working diligently to silence political opposition by suppressing social media, imposing strict Internet and instant messaging regulations, and banning academic research and teaching on topics such as civil society, universal values, citizens' rights, freedom of the press, independence of the judiciary, and capitalism.

In 2013, China unilaterally imposed an air defense identification zone over the East China Sea, imposing unnecessary risk to international civilian air traffic. Less than 1 year later, China turned a tin ear to its neighbors concerns by placing a drilling platform in disputed waters off Vietnam. Around the same time, Chinese naval vessels and its air force began to behave aggressively attempting to intimidate U.S. naval vessels and aircraft operating in international waters and airspace.

Many consider current U.S.-China relations to have reached the lowest point in a decade. And, amazingly, there is no senior administration official that leads the China portfolio. So it comes as no surprise that the Obama administration's response to Hong Kong's cry for help did so little to instill confidence with the people of Hong Kong.

The U.S. must never stand idle when democracy is being challenged. When the glow of press conferences has faded, we must remember that what is happening in Hong Kong is not an isolated event. President Xi is dismantling the ''One Country, Two System'' governance arrangement—a strategy orchestrated by Beijing that certainly has put our friend and ally Taiwan on notice that any accommodation or agreement may be revoked at moment's notice and is not worth the paper it is written on.

If the Obama administration is so serious about its pivot to Asia, how can it go so long without offering credible support to the people of Hong Kong and their democratic aspirations, which are in fact written and promised in law? Saying that the U.S. does not take sides in the political development of Hong Kong and doesn't support any particular individuals or groups involved, as the U.S. Consulate in Hong Kong stated, is not acceptable or correct for that matter. This response is a capitulation to China and abandonment of our promises to Hong Kong that U.S. support of democratization in Hong Kong is a fundamental principle of U.S. foreign policy, as are the human rights of the people of Hong Kong.

While hundreds and thousands of protesters have stood their ground against attacks by thuggish China Communist Party supporters and waves of tear gas and pepper spray from police, the Obama administration has stood on the sidelines. Are the wishes of the Hong Kong people not clear enough? And after a period of calm, protests are once again escalating, and nearly 200 people have been arrested, including many of the Umbrella Movement's leaders. Now is not the time to remain silent and reticent in support for Hong Kong's democratic future. The U.S.-Hong Kong Policy Act of 1992 states that the U.S. should play an active role in maintaining Hong Kong's confidence and prosperity. These aspirations are progressively diminishing as a result of China's growing control over Hong Kong's Government and the civil rights of its people.

We are at a pivotal moment for democracy in Hong Kong. No matter how long China tries to suppress basic human rights, ban the pursuit of democratic ideals, and quash civil society, we must not let Beijing succeed in destroying the values the people in Hong Kong are fighting so hard to keep. The Obama administration needs to more vocally support the pro-democratic aspirations of the Hong Kong people. We must not let Beijing's accusations of foreign influence bully us into silence over upholding human rights and supporting the right of the Hong Kong people to choose their own political future.

The U.S.-Hong Kong Policy Act stipulates differential treatment of Hong Kong only as long as it is considered sufficiently autonomous from China. Considering Beijing's orchestration of the Hong Kong Government's responses to the crises, and dictation over who can and cannot enter or leave Hong Kong, it may be time to reassess Hong Kong's autonomous status, and those benefits that come with that status.

I thank our witnesses for being here this afternoon. We look forward to hearing your thoughts on how the situation in Hong Kong may evolve in the coming weeks and months. I now recognize our ranking member, Mr. Faleomavaega, for his opening remarks.

Mr. FALEOMAVAEGA. Thank you, Mr. Chairman. I thank you for holding this timely hearing in light of the serious protests in response to conditions set by China for the 2017 elections for Hong Kong's Chief Executive.

For years, Mr. Chairman, I have been critical of our U.S. foreign policy toward the Asia-Pacific region. While not taking anything less of importance as far as Europe and the Middle East is concerned, I have always said that we are not paying enough attention to the Asia-Pacific region, especially when two-thirds of the world's population is in the Asia-Pacific region. You can talk about the armies, you can talk about the economics, and I think it is well said.

As President Ma states, Hong Kong is an extremely important global financial center, and any political turmoil that occurs there will impact not only Asia but the entire world. President Ma points out that Taiwan has had universal suffrage for some time, and believes that if a system of universal suffrage can be realized in Hong Kong, both Hong Kong as well as Mainland China would benefit.

I would add, Mr. Chairman, that the Asia-Pacific region and the United States would also benefit, as would the entire world. I ask to include President Ma's statement in the record for the historical purposes.

Mr. CHABOT. Without objection, so ordered.

Mr. FALEOMAVAEGA. As this will be my last subcommittee hearing, I want the publicly express my appreciation for you, Mr. Chairman. I have served as both chairman and ranking member of this subcommittee, and I have served with many others over the years. One of my most cherished honors has been serving with you. You, as a member of the committee, Chairman Chabot, are a loyal and principled man who serves your constituents in the Asia-Pacific region with distinction and honor. No matter where I go from here, I will always take your friendship with me. I am going to miss you.

I am also going to miss each and every member of this subcommittee who served with us, including my dear friend Dana Rohrabacher, who is my buddy, truly my buddy. I especially thank Mr. Bera for the gracious support he and his staff provided by filling in for me during my time of recovery.

I also want to pay special tribute to Kevin and Priscilla. You chose well when you chose those as staff director and professional staffs, respectively. I am deeply appreciative of the support they have given to you and me and to my staff as well. Their knowledge and expertise in the Asia-Pacific region has influenced many, and I will remember them both for their extraordinary goodness, and I know that my staff feels the same way toward them.

So, Mr. Chairman, to you, to our subcommittee members and staff, I extend my highest and kindest regards. May God be with each of you till we meet again. Soifua.

Mr. CHABOT. Thank you very much. Thank you very much.

If the gentleman from Pennsylvania wouldn't mind if we go out of order and have Mr. Rohrabacher speak now. Gentleman from California is recognized.

Mr. ROHRABACHER. Thank you very much. And this is, of course, a very symbolic hearing today in that we are discussing how important the Pacific and the Asia and Pacific Rim is to the United States of America, and how the people there on that part of the world need to know that we are paying attention that we are on the side of those people who are struggling to make the word a better place. And here it is, the last day, Eni's last day, a man who has been working all these years.

And how many years altogether, Eni?

Mr. FALEOMAVAEGA. Too many.

Mr. ROHRABACHER. Too many. Well, I think I was 24 when we were running overseas in all kind of wild places in the world.

But Eni has dedicated his life, from the time he was a young soldier in Vietnam till this very moment, toward making this a better world. And while we have had a few disagreements, we have also shared the great common value of a commitment to making it a better and freer world, and toward bringing the people of the Pacific and of Asia into that type of relationship with the people of the United States.

So, Eni, God bless you and Godspeed.

Just a few thoughts about this hearing.

I think one of the greatest mistakes that was ever made by any President of the United States in my lifetime was made by a Republican President, Herbert Walker Bush. After Ronald Reagan cleared the path toward a great expansion of democracy, and China at that time seemed to be heading toward democracy, Herbert Walker Bush betrayed the people in Tiananmen Square, betrayed the democratic movement, and let them be slaughtered. We never did we have the retaliation against this evil regime in Beijing that we should have had after Tiananmen Square. We would have had a far better world today had the democracy movement won at that time. Herbert Walker Bush was to blame for that loss. Instead, we have a government that is the world's worst human rights abuser.

But today, we send a message to the young pro-democracy activists now in the streets of Hong Kong: You are not alone. We think of you. We are with you. All people have the right to be free. But it has to be earned. And today we recognize the brave young men and women in the streets of Hong Kong who are earning their freedom, earning their right to democracy, and to control their own destiny through the ballot box.

So today we say to the young people in Hong Kong, we are with you, don't fear, and we will try our best not to make the mistake that we made at Tiananmen Square. This time we stand strong for our values. And even though Eni won't be with us to make sure that we are keeping that promise, I can assure you that he will be behind us, giving us telephone calls, and thus we meet our responsibility.

So thank you very much, Eni.

And thank you, Mr. Chairman, for this hearing.

Mr. CHABOT. Thank you very much. Gentleman's time has expired.

Gentleman from California, Mr. Bera, is recognized.

Mr. BERA. I will just maybe some brief comments.

When we look at Hong Kong, when we look at the protests that are taking place, when we look at the promise of the 1997 treaty, I am interested in hearing the witnesses' testimony and getting to the bottom of how this transition is taking place and getting to a point where we can get to one person, one vote and you have a true democracy. Because ultimately at the foundation of freedom and democracy is the ability to express your voice through your votes and pick your own leadership.

So I am curious to see how that transition is going, where we are today, and how we get to where we want to be in 2017. So I am looking forward to that testimony. Thank you.

Mr. CHABOT. Thank you very much.

The gentleman from Arizona is recognized.

Mr. SALMON. Thank you.

First and foremost, I want to echo the sentiments that have been expressed toward Mr. Faleomavaega. This is my second opportunity serving with him, once was in the 1990s and now again. There has never been a more tireless supporter of the indigent peoples of various nations than Mr. Faleomavaega.

And we are going to really miss you. You are a wonderful man and your heart is a good one and you have always strived to do the right thing, not the partisan thing, and I appreciate that.

As far as Hong Kong is concerned, I was there for the handover ceremony of Hong Kong from Great Britain to China and met with Martin Lee and other folks that were very, very dubious about what would happen with this "One Country, Two Systems" that China was proposing. And I am sad to say that some of those fears that Mr. Lee expressed at that time have been realized. That Beijing, who has said that they were going to let Hong Kong be autonomous, then puts down all their rules and regulations about how the vetting process is going to be done by Beijing to decide who gets to run and who doesn't.

I congratulate these young people for standing up for freedom and standing up for their beliefs. It is not always easy. And I want to echo the sentiments of Mr. Rohrabacher. We need to be strong in our response in defending freedom anywhere across the globe. And if these young people run into harm's way, let our voice and our actions be very, very clear that we are on the side of freedom and democracy.

And I yield back the balance of my time.

Mr. CHABOT. Thank you very much. Gentlemen's time has expired.

The gentleman from California is recognized.

Mr. SHERMAN. Mr. Chairman, it was good to be with you, Dana Rohrabacher, and of course the chairman of the committee back in February in Hong Kong where we had a chance to meet those who have really devoted their lives to trying to give democracy to the Hong Kong people.

We had a chance to meet with Martin Lee, just as the gentleman from Arizona met with him at the time that this all began, when we were promised "One Country, Two Systems." But when it came to political rights and freedoms, it looks like it is one country, one system. One person, one vote, and one committee that decides who you are allowed to vote for.

I think that we should speak out in favor of the Hong Kong people. But let us be frank. We can't take military action. We are unlikely to take trade action. And oratorical support is the most we can provide or are likely to provide. But as we negotiate so many transactions with China, we should remember that the promise to millions of its own citizens has been broken and we should be very careful in transacting business with a country that has behaved like this.

Finally, if China thinks that Taiwan would voluntarily reunite with the mainland, I don't think the slogan they are going to use is "One Country, Two Systems." I think that slogan has been tarnished.

Mr. CHABOT. Thank you very much. Gentleman's time has expired.

The gentleman from Pennsylvania, Mr. Perry, is recognized.

Mr. PERRY. Thanks, Mr. Chairman. I just want to say I appreciate this hearing on this very timely and important subject. I look forward to the testimony of the presenters here today. I think today is a good time to think about our pivot or our alleged pivot as a Nation to Asia and what that means. Today I also think about the cost of freedom, how it must be earned and won and how it must be renewed. Today I also want to reiterate how fragile democracy is, and the freedom that we experience, that we love and cherish today. By watching the events in Hong Kong, especially, you can tell that it won't be taken away in one fell swoop, but by increments. We can learn a lot from that in our own society today.

So I am very much looking forward to the answers and the questions regarding this.

And with that, Mr. Chairman, I yield back.

Mr. CHABOT. Thank you. The gentleman yields back.

Are there any other members that seek to make an opening statement? If not, we will go ahead and introduce our panel here this afternoon.

We will begin with Dean Cheng, who serves as a senior research fellow in the Asian Studies Center at the Davis Institute for National Security and Foreign Policy at the Heritage Foundation. His portfolio includes Chinese political and security affairs with an emphasis on China's military policy and U.S.-China policy. He previously worked as a senior analyst for Science Applications International Corps, where he handled defense and homeland security issues. He also worked with the China Studies Division of the Center for Naval Analysis. Before that, Mr. Cheng served as a China defense analyst for the Office of Technology Assessment's International Security and Space Program, where he studied China's defense-industrial complex. Mr. Cheng has provided analysis for a number of news media sources and is a contributor to the BBC World Service, National Public Radio, Washington Post, and Time magazine, amongst others. Mr. Cheng is a regular speaker on China defense issues and U.S.-China policy. Mr. Cheng holds a bachelor's degree in political science from Princeton University and studied for a doctorate at the Massachusetts Institute of Technology.

We welcome you here this afternoon.

Our next witness will be Sophie Richardson, who serves as the China director at Human Rights Watch. Dr. Richardson is the author of numerous articles on domestic Chinese political reform, democratization, and human rights in Asia. She has previously testified before the European Parliament and both the U.S. House of Representatives and the U.S. Senate. She provides regular commentary to news media outlets. In 2009, Dr. Richardson, published the book ''China, Cambodia, and the Five Principles of Peaceful Coexistence.'' Dr. Richardson has received degrees from the University of Virginia, Johns Hopkins School of Advanced International Studies, Hopkins-Nanjing Program, and Oberlin College. And we welcome you this afternoon, Doctor.

Lastly, our final witness is Kelley Currie, who is a senior fellow with the Project 2049 Institute. Her portfolio includes democracy, human rights, and the rule of law in the Asia-Pacific region. Prior to joining Project 2049, Ms. Currie served as an Asia policy advisor to the Under Secretary of State for Democracy and Global Affairs and Special Coordinator for Tibetan Issues, Paula Dobriansky. She has also served as senior advisor to the International Committee of the Red Cross, director of Government Relations for the International Campaign for Tibet, and deputy director for Asia at International Republican Institute. Ms. Currie was the foreign policy advisor to Congressman John Porter and concurrently served as the majority staff director of the Congressional Human Rights Caucus. Ms. Currie received a JD from Georgetown University Law Center and an undergraduate degree in political science from the University of Georgia School of Public and International Affairs. She has appeared as an expert commentator on CNN and the BBC and has written on Asia policy issues for national and international publications.

We welcome all three of you here this afternoon. We look forward to your testimony. I am sure you are all familiar with the 5-minute rule. You will each have 5 minutes to testify. A yellow light will come on letting you know you have 1 minute, and the red light tells you to wrap up, if at all possible. We give you a little leeway but not a whole lot.

Dr. Cheng, you are recognized for 5 minutes.

STATEMENT OF MR. DEAN CHENG, SENIOR RESEARCH FELLOW, ASIAN STUDIES CENTER, THE DAVIS INSTITUTE FOR NATIONAL SECURITY AND FOREIGN POLICY, THE HERITAGE FOUNDATION

Mr. CHENG. Chairman Chabot, distinguished members of the committee, thank you for the opportunity to be here this afternoon. Ranking Member Faleomavaega, thank you for the fortuitous opportunity to address you on your last session here. My comments today are my own and should not be construed as representing any official position of the Heritage Foundation.

Since the 1980s, when the U.K. Began negotiating with the People's Republic of China over the return of Hong Kong, the territory has been something like the proverbial canary in the coal mine. How Beijing would handle this territory and its population of 7 million would reflect broader issues of internal Chinese governance, cross-straits relations with Taiwan, and prospects for the broader Asia-Pacific region.

Key questions here were, could the PRC allow pluralism to exist within the context of its political system, which is dominated by the Chinese Communist Party? Would it allow Hong Kong to continue to flourish after it had been returned to Chinese sovereignty? And might Hong Kong serve as a bridge for a modernizing, increasingly wealthy PRC to liberalize itself?

In this regard, Hong Kong was seen as the perfect experiment. In the first place, Hong Kong already enjoyed certain key institutions, including a free press, an independent judiciary, and the rule of law. Beijing would not have to create these from whole cloth. Instead, it merely needed to allow the system within Hong Kong to continue and not interfere.

To further reinforce this point, the PRC was also obligated to respect Hong Kong. The Joint Declaration between London and Beijing, as well as the Basic Law of Hong Kong, were both formal obligations undertaken by the PRC that guaranteed Hong Kong's system for 50 years. These documents were seen as codifying the idea of ''One Country, Two Systems,'' the principle under which Hong Kong was to be returned to Chinese sovereignty yet retain its own characteristics.

Finally, there was the assessment of enlightened self-interest. Hong Kong was already a major financial hub and a major economy in its own right when it reverted to Chinese control. Nor was there any question that after 1997 that Hong Kong was, in fact, under Chinese control. The PRC was, therefore, seen as having every reason to want it to succeed, and it was presumed would therefore not interfere with its operation.

Fast forward 17 years and the Chinese position regarding universal suffrage and how the Hong Kong Special Administrative Region would select its Chief Executive in 2017 suggests that, unfortunately, these assumptions and views were far too optimistic. China has gone from a still-developing country in 1997 to the world's second-largest economy, and in the process its attitude toward Hong Kong and indeed toward much of the region has hardened.

As the June Chinese white paper on Hong Kong made clear, Beijing now emphasizes the ''one country'' part of ''One Country, Two Systems,'' and made also clear that Hong Kong will maintain its own system only at Beijing's sufferance.

China's approach to Hong Kong as seen in the suffrage issue highlights several key areas of concern. First, there is little reason to expect political reform in the PRC for the foreseeable future. Some had hoped that Xi Jinping might be a closet political reformer, but his approach to Hong Kong hardly supports this view. Instead, his handling of the Hong Kong situation with little violence and certainly no repetition of the scenes and costs associated with Tiananmen Square, now 25 ago, has probably strengthened his domestic credibility, helped in his consolidation of power, but given him little reason to liberalize his policies.

Second, China is demonstrating once again its aptitude for political warfare. Political warfare is the hardest form have soft power. Much as Russia has employed hybrid or ambiguous warfare in its Crimea intervention, China is doing the same in Hong Kong and elsewhere in the region. And in particular, we can see the exercising of the three warfares: Legal warfare or lawfare, public opinion warfare, and psychological warfare.

China's approach to the franchise and suffrage in Hong Kong has been consistent with its writings on legal warfare, which focus on the use of the law as an instrument for justifying or furthering national aims. This is a much more offensive approach, employing the law to achieve previously established ends rather than defensively limiting or otherwise constraining one's own activities.

This lawfare approach also complements Chinese public opinion warfare methods. Social and news media in China are tightly controlled by the government, and once the protests began, Chinese Weibo messages, the local equivalent of Twitter, were immediately censored.

Meanwhile, the harassment of Hong Kong activists is integral to Chinese psychological warfare methods. The fact that even the average protester has been detained or had their travels limited serves notice that anyone who protests has likely been recorded and will suffer consequences.

Third, this approach to Hong Kong, and especially the ''One Country, Two Systems'', the way it is now defined, is likely to lead to greater tensions with Taiwan. The approach of ''One Country, Two Systems'' was always intended to appeal the people of Taiwan to persuade them to accept reunification, but the message from recent events in Hong Kong is a cautionary, not an encouraging tale.

For the United States, this has three implications. China's assiduous practice of political warfare is a warning about engaging the PRC without carefully thinking through all of the angles. We should engage the PRC much as we approach contract talks, with no assumption of shared outlooks, although both sides are interested in reaching an agreement and avoiding a strike.

In addition, the prospect of heightened tensions across the Taiwan Straits means that the Asia pivot needs to be made more meaningful. This includes the Trans-Pacific Partnership Trade Agreement to underscore that America offers more than military solutions.

But one final element is to strengthen the American military presence, including a more robust training and exercise schedule with friends and allies, but also expanding the provision of more advanced equipment to those same friends and allies, whether it is missile defense cooperation with Japan and South Korea, military sales to Vietnam, or acting on the sale of fighter aircraft and submarines to Taiwan.

Thank you very much.

Mr. CHABOT. Thank you very much.

[The prepared statement of Mr. Cheng follows:]

214 Massachusetts Avenue, NE • Washington DC 20002 • (202) 546-4400 • heritage.org

CONGRESSIONAL TESTIMONY

The Implications of Hong Kong Protests for the United States

Testimony before the Committee on Foreign Affairs United States House of Representatives

December 2, 2014

Dean Cheng
Senior Research Fellow
The Heritage Foundation

Thank you, Chairman Chabot, Ranking Member Faleomavaega, and distinguished members of the Subcommittee for the opportunity to be here today.

My name is Dean Cheng. I am the Senior Research Fellow for Chinese Political and Security Affairs at The Heritage Foundation. The views I express in this testimony are my own and should not be construed as representing any official position of The Heritage Foundation.

My comments here today will discuss the impact of recent Chinese actions in Hong Kong on the American security posture in the western Pacific.

Introduction

Hong Kong has long been a test case for the People's Republic of China (PRC), and also an indicator for Sino-American relations. The reversion of Hong Kong from British rule to Chinese control was seen as a demonstration of the viability of the "one country, two systems" approach.

At base, Hong Kong is a test of whether the PRC can be sufficiently flexible to allow some pluralism. A successful transition would indicate that China was a pragmatic power that was likely to evolve and be able to incorporate alternative approaches, within a system that would remain dominated by the Chinese Communist Party (CCP). Beijing, and some in Washington, saw it as the potential way to a peaceful resolution of the Taiwan issue. Developments in Hong Kong mean that "one country, two systems" is likely permanently off the table as a settlement approach for cross-strait relations. In fact, any kind of political reconciliation between the PRC and Taiwan has been set back for the foreseeable future. This, in turn, has obvious implications for the United States, given the commitment Washington has made to ensuring that the future of Taiwan is determined through peaceful means. Furthermore, because Hong Kong was already a wealthy community when it transitioned to Chinese control, the reversion would also be a test to see whether China was likely to become a society that would respond to increasing wealth with a concomitant demand for greater political freedom—and whether Beijing would be able to handle such demands. In this regard, given the status of Hong Kong as a major global financial center, China would have additional incentives to ensure the community's stability and credibility.

In this regard, China found itself in the happy position of coming to control a self-contained environment, where a variety of key institutions and structures were already in place, including an independent judiciary, a free press, and a tradition of the rule of law. Consequently, China would not even have to create such precedents out of whole cloth, but would primarily have to administer a ready-made structure.

The Hong Kong Protests

Hong Kong island was ceded to Great Britain in perpetuity at the end of the First Opium War, in 1842, followed by Kowloon Peninsula in 1860 at the end of the Second Opium War. The New Territories of Lantau Island and the area up to the Shenzhen River were leased to Great Britain for 99 years in 1898. Because the three portions of Hong Kong (Hong Kong island, Kowloon, and the New Territories) were effectively integrated, the return of only the last portion was not feasible. Consequently, Great Britain and the PRC negotiated for the return of the combined territory to China. The two key documents governing this reversion were the Joint Declaration of the Government of the United Kingdom of Great Britain and Northern Ireland and the Government of the People's Republic of China on the Question of Hong Kong, and the Basic Law of Hong Kong.

The governing principle for what would become the Hong Kong Special Administrative Region (HKSAR) would be "one country, two systems." Sovereignty over Hong Kong was to revert to the PRC, but the people of Hong Kong were to be granted a high degree of autonomy in all matters other than foreign policy and defense. They would be allowed to operate under capitalist market economics, and more open political systems, even though these would be significantly different from the socialist market economy and Communist Party–led system of the PRC. This separate status, including a free press and an independent judiciary, would be ensured for fifty years.

What was also made clear in the Basic Law, however, was that interpretation of the law was in the hands of the Standing Committee of the National People's Congress (NPC) of the PRC. This is consistent with the Chinese constitution, which designated the NPC as "the highest organ of state power."

While there was agreement on the "ultimate aim" of universal suffrage in the selection of Hong Kong's Chief Executive and Legislative Council, how that would be implemented remained uncertain.

Beijing's sentiments were most explicitly expressed, however, in an unprecedented "white paper" on Hong Kong, released in June 2014. The white paper made clear that "two systems" was subordinate to the idea of "one country." Hong Kong, the paper admonished, needed to understand that it exists as part of the PRC, and any rights and privileges it enjoys are derived from the central authorities in Beijing.

> The high degree of autonomy of the HKSAR is not full autonomy, nor a decentralized power. It is the power to run local affairs as authorized by the central leadership. The high degree of autonomy of HKSAR is subject to the level of the central leadership's authorization. There is no such thing called "residual power." …The most important thing to do in upholding the "one country" principle is to maintain China's sovereignty, security and development interests, and respect the country's fundamental system and other systems and principles.
>
> The "two systems" means that, within the "one country" the main body of the country practices socialism, while Hong Kong and some other regions practice capitalism. The "one country" is the premise and basis of the "two systems," and the "two systems" is subordinate to and derived from "one country."[1]

---

[1] State Council Information Office, *The Practice of the "One Country, Two Systems" Policy in the Hong Kong Special Administrative Region* (Beijing, PRC: State Council Information Office, 2014),

In August 2014, the Chinese authorities unveiled their plan for selecting the HKSAR Chief Executive in 2017. While the citizens of Hong Kong would be allowed to cast votes, their selection would be among a slate of two to three candidates determined by a China-dominated nominating committee. This approach would ensure, as the NPC noted, "the long-term prosperity and stability of Hong Kong and the sovereignty, security and development interests of the country." As important, it ensured that the Chief Executive would be "a person who loves the country and loves Hong Kong." This, it was noted, was a "basic requirement of the policy of 'one country, two systems.'"[2] In essence, citizens of Hong Kong would be allowed to vote, but whom they could vote for would essentially be pre-determined by Beijing, because Hong Kong is fundamentally part of China.

The combination of the white paper, the decision, and the associated statement by the NPC led to a variety of reactions. Among the Hong Kong business elite, overwhelmingly concerned about maintaining stability and a good working relationship with Beijing, there was more concern about protests than about the PRC decision.[3] Some pro-Beijing elements argue that the right to vote is explicit, but that does not extend to public nominations.[4] Pro-democracy elements countered that Beijing's decision effectively neutered the voice of the people of Hong Kong, and promised to oppose the framework; since any framework requires a two-thirds majority, this would effectively veto any change.[5]

The situation escalated in late September, when thousands of students began to boycott classes. This was followed by some of the largest demonstrations the territory had seen in years, organized by a variety of groups including "Occupy Central with Love and Peace." The protests were initially met by a controlled police response, with various protestors arrested and then released, but on September 28, the police employed large amounts of tear gas and much more force to break up the demonstrations. The result was popular revulsion, and far larger demonstrations that eventually led to large numbers of demonstrators occupying parts of Central and Admiralty districts in downtown Hong Kong.

In the intervening two months since the protestors first massed in downtown Hong Kong, the situation has remained relatively calm. The protestors have gone to great pains to avoid claiming that they are interested in either revolution or independence, recognizing that any such implication would likely lead to a far more violent reaction from Beijing. As one organizer took

---

http://www.scmp.com/news/hong-kong/article/1529167/full-text-practice-one-country-two-systems-policy-hong-kong-special.

[2] Standing Committee of the National People's Congress. "Decision of the Standing Committee of the National People's Congress on Issues Relating to the Selection of the Chief Executive of the Hong Kong Special Administrative Region by Universal Suffrage and on the Method for Forming the Legislative Council of the Hong Kong Special Administrative Region in the Year 2016" (Beijing, PRC: National People's Congress, August 31, 2014), http://news.xinhuanet.com/english/china/2014-08/31/c_133609238_2.htm.

[3] See Kit Tang, "Will 'Occupy Central' Hurt Hong Kong?" CNBC, June 24, 2014, http://www.cnbc.com/id/101786534#.

[4] Juliana Lu. "Hong Kong Protests: Did China Go Back on Its Promises?" BBC, October 2, 2014, http://www.bbc.com/news/world-asia-china-29454385.

[5] Richard Bush, "China's Decision on Universal Suffrage in Hong Kong." Brookings Institution Up Front blog, September 2, 2014, http://www.brookings.edu/blogs/up-front/posts/2014/09/02-hong-kong-chief-executive-election-bush.

pains to point out, "This is not a color revolution."[6] Similarly, they have not occupied government offices.

For its part, Beijing has no interest in staging another Tiananmen Massacre. Beijing has been willing to leave the situation up to Hong Kong authorities to handle; indeed, all of the police forces employed thus far have been from the Hong Kong Police Force, with no evidence of participation by military or police forces from the mainland. At the same time, however, Beijing has given no indication that it will compromise in any way or engage in any meaningful negotiations.

As important, the Chinese authorities have worked assiduously to limit coverage of the Hong Kong protests in the Chinese press and social media. Within hours of the initial protests, Weibo, China's version of Twitter, was actively censoring traffic. Meanwhile, the photo-sharing service Instagram was also shut down.[7] Chinese efforts to restrict discussion and news about Hong Kong developments helped limit support from Chinese for the demonstrations—which has not appeared strong to begin with.[8]

The resulting stalemate has meant the protests have slowly receded from the public consciousness, as the number of protestors has dwindled. After two months of protesting, there is far more limited coverage by local and international news media. While some major figures, such as Jimmy Lai, a Hong Kong media figure and major businessman, remain committed, independent polls suggest that many Hong Kong citizens see the protests as futile.[9] Hong Kong authorities have begun to dismantle some of the barricades, with little opposition from the protestors.[10] There have been dozens of arrests, including prominent student leaders.

Beijing, however, has also indicated that its decision not to employ force directly does not mean that it has not been paying attention to the protestors. Activists who participated in some of the protests are now apparently being denied entry into China. This has included not only leaders, but also "relative unknowns — not leaders — who merely participated in the protests, which included hundreds of thousands of others."[11] It would not be surprising if, in the future, key protestors were detained, and all known protestors are likely to be subject to surveillance for a long time to come.

---

[6] Helen Regan, "Hong Kong Protestors Urge Reform, Not Revolution," *Time*, October 5, 2014, http://time.com/3469493/watch-hong-kong-protest-leaders-urge-reform-not-revolution/.

[7] "China 'Censors Hong Kong Protests Posts on Social Media,'" BBC, September 29, 2014. http://www.bbc.com/news/world-asia-china-29411270.

[8] Frank Langfitt, "On China's Mainland, A Less Charitable Take on Hong Kong's Protests," NPR. October 6, 2014. http://www.npr.org/blogs/parallels/2014/10/06/354088313/on-chinas-mainland-a-less-charitable-take-on-hong-kongs-protests

[9] Frank Langfitt, "After Two Months, Hong Kong Residents Want Protestors to Head Home," NPR, November 23, 2014, http://www.npr.org/blogs/parallels/2014/11/23/365995044/after-two-months-hong-kong-residents-want-protesters-to-head-home.

[10] Kelvin Chan, "Hong Kong Government Starts Dismantling Protest Barricades." *The Christian Science Monitor*, November 17, 2014, http://www.csmonitor.com/World/Latest-News-Wires/2014/1117/Hong-Kong-government-starts-dismantling-protest-barricades-video.

[11] William Wan and Kris Cheng Lok-Chit." Hong Kong Protestors Denied Entry into China," *The Washington Post*, November 24, 2014, http://www.washingtonpost.com/world/asia_pacific/hong-kong-protesters-denied-entry-into-china/2014/11/23/0ed9618c-70c4-11e4-a2c2-478179fd0489_story.html .

Implications of the Protests for the PRC

Perhaps the greatest impact of the Hong Kong protests has been on President Xi Jinping. Xi has both gained and lost from developments in the HKSAR.

Xi benefited from the events in Hong Kong, because *he successfully dealt with the first externally driven major crisis to confront him* since he acceded to power in 2012. In the other situations that have arisen during his first two years in power, much of the tempo of the crisis was driven by Chinese actions. This is consistent with the apparent Chinese view that, in most crises, they have the ability to manipulate the crisis to a fairly high degree.

Thus, the tensions and confrontations that ensued after China deployed the deep sea drilling platform Haiyang Shiyou 981 (HY-981) into disputed waters between China and Vietnam were ultimately under Chinese control.[12] When the Chinese withdrew the rig in July, after nearly two months of operation, Hanoi did not sustain the crisis. Similarly, in the recent border confrontation between China and India, where China moved hundreds of troops into Indian-controlled territory on the eve of President Xi's visit to India, Beijing was confident that it was in control of the situation.[13] Although the Chinese military presence dampened the premier meeting between Xi and Indian Prime Minister Modi, the Chinese apparently did not fear that such a move might precipitate a broader confrontation.

In the case of Hong Kong, however, the impetus for these tensions arose from the people of Hong Kong. They actively opposed the political dictates issued from Beijing, in a manner that Beijing could not easily ratchet up or down. While Beijing could employ force, it was clear that this was not the preferred option; consequently, Beijing was compelled to rely upon the authorities in the Hong Kong government to resolve the situation. In having to operate through intermediaries, China's ability to directly control the outcome was even more limited.

Nonetheless, the crisis has been, at this point, apparently resolved. Moreover, it has not involved any casualties or significant property damage; nor has it necessitated the employment of violent force, nor the deployment of reinforcements from the mainland. Indeed, the disruptions to Hong Kong's business and financial centers has been marginal. Certainly, it has not resulted in the devastation to Hong Kong's, China's, or Xi Jinping's reputation had there been a repetition of the heavy-handed response that marked Tiananmen Square 25 years ago. Consequently, Xi Jinping can reasonably argue that his effective leadership, including a willingness to trust subordinates, has resulted in a generally acceptable resolution of the situation.

This underscores Xi's ongoing consolidation of power, which has already seen him bring down not only General Xu Caihou, a former Vice Chairman of the powerful Central Military Commission (CMC), but also topple Zhou Yongkang. Not only was Zhou the former head of the

---

[12] Ankit Panda, "Why Did China Set Up an Oil Rig In Vietnamese Waters?" *The Diplomat*, May 13, 2014, http://thediplomat.com/2014/05/why-did-china-set-up-an-oil-rig-within-vietnamese-waters/; Jane Perlez, "Chinese Oil Rig Near Vietnam To Be Moved," *The New York Times*, July 15, 2014, http://www.nytimes.com/2014/07/16/world/asia/chinese-oil-rig-near-vietnam-to-be-moved.html.

[13] Sanjeev Miglani, "India Says to Defend China Border After Standoff Ahead of Xi Visit," Reuters, September 16. 2014, http://www.reuters.com/article/2014/09/16/us-india-china-border-idUSKBN0HB0MZ20140916; Shannon Tiezzi, "China, India End Military Standoff Along Disputed Border," *The Diplomat*, October 1, 2014, http://thediplomat.com/2014/10/china-india-end-military-stand-off-along-disputed-border/.

Ministry of Public Security, but more importantly, he was a former member of the Politburo Standing Committee, and therefore one of the 10 most powerful men in the PRC. Xi is arguably more firmly ensconced in power two years into his tenure than Hu Jintao or Jiang Zemin (his two predecessors) were at corresponding points in their leadership.

The (thus far) successful resolution of the Hong Kong crisis also has *preserved Hong Kong's status and credibility as a major economic center*. Had there been sustained violence or an extended disruption of Hong Kong's activities, it would have likely called into question the city's viability as a global financial hub. If the PRC is to successfully open its capital accounts, on the way to establishing a credible commercial banking system, it would likely have to rely on the expertise resident in Hong Kong's gleaming towers. Such a transition is essential in dealing with China's burgeoning bad debt problem. A violence-wracked city would likely have seen a significant brain drain.

Xi lost from the events in Hong Kong, because *Beijing's high-handed approach to Hong Kong democracy, as expressed in the white paper and NPC statement, have revealed the limitations of the "one country, two systems" approach*. But "one country, two systems" was always primarily focused on Taiwan, as an enticement to persuade the people on that island to accept reunification with the mainland. A successful integration of Hong Kong into the larger Chinese polity would provide clear evidence that Taiwan, too, could find a place within the larger PRC. But the explicit emphasis of "one country" over "two systems," as well as the legalistic arguments that effectively nullified the franchise in the HKSAR, limit any appeal of the idea of reunification.

The Hong Kong protests, moreover, occur as *some in Taiwan are already reassessing cross-strait relations*. In March and April, the Sunflower movement, a student-led organization, occupied the Taiwan legislature in opposition to a China-Taiwan free trade agreement in services.[14] Arguing that the Cross-Strait Service Trade Agreement (CSSTA) had been reached in secret, that it posed risks to Taiwan's national security, and that it would lead to a massive influx of cheap Chinese labor, the movement mobilized some 100,000 protestors, one of the largest such outpourings in the island's history. Before the protestors eventually left the legislature in May, they extracted a promise from the head of the legislature to establish a watchdog process that would assess the national security implications of any new trade deals.[15] Consequently, the CSSTA remains in limbo.

For those already concerned about the PRC, *the Chinese approach to Hong Kong only justifies and reinforces their skepticism*. Indeed, there is arguably growing resistance to expanding either economic or political linkages across the strait. This may be reflected in the 2016 elections in Taiwan. The incumbent president, Ma Ying-jeou, is completing his second term, and cannot run for office again. Despite being reelected in 2012, Ma's low polling numbers, coupled with an economic slow-down and various scandals, jeopardize the Kuomintang (KMT) party's hold on power. Support from the Sunflower movement may result in a win by the Democratic Progressive Party (DPP), which is much more in favor of independence for Taiwan. This, in turn, would likely pose a major challenge to Xi and the Chinese leadership, who have enjoyed a

---

[14] J.R., "Sunflower Sutra," *The Economist*, April 8, 2014,
http://www.economist.com/blogs/banyan/2014/04/politics-taiwan.

[15] Kirsty Needham, "Sunflower Power Stalls Trade Deal," *The Sydney Morning Herald*, November 22, 2014,
http://www.smh.com.au/world/sunflower-power-stalls-taiwan-trade-deal-20141122-11rl8d.html.

quiescent relationship with President Ma and the Taipei government since 2008. Meanwhile, President Ma has voiced support for the Hong Kong protestors.[16]

A key lesson that the PRC leadership has likely drawn from the results in Hong Kong is the *importance of political warfare*, as a means of managing and controlling the discourse. Political warfare (*zhengzhi zuozhan*) is a form of combat that encompasses all methods of non-military strikes, employing political, theoretical/ideological, morale, and psychological means of conflict. From the Chinese perspective, political warfare should be considered *the hardest form of soft power*. The aim of political warfare is to secure the political initiative and psychological advantage over an opponent, in order to strengthen one's own will, secure sympathy from third parties, and debilitate an opponent. It is targeted as much at one's own population as foreigners, and does not occur only in time of formal hostilities. From the Chinese perspective, the events in downtown Hong Kong constituted a political warfare battleground.

Consequently, the PRC waged "the three warfares," public opinion warfare, legal warfare, and psychological warfare, against the demonstrators, in order to achieve its ends of manageable disruption and limiting support in the HKSAR, while avoiding the use of military force. The events in Hong Kong would seem to confirm the Chinese view that *public opinion warfare* is sufficiently important that it is a constant, ongoing activity, aimed at long-term influence of perceptions and attitudes.

Beijing conducted public opinion warfare by controlling the mass information channels, including television, radio, news organizations, but especially social media. The clamp-down on reporting about developments within China, coupled with the state controlled media, meant that not only did the vast majority of Chinese not know about the protests, but that what little they did learn was from Beijing's point of view. This allowed Beijing to shape the Chinese public's perception of what was going on. As important, by depriving the protestors of the prospect of support within China, it sapped the morale of the local protestors.

China, meanwhile, has been more broadly clamping down on foreign media. Beijing has issued directives limiting cooperation between Chinese and foreign journalists, refused visas to some foreign correspondents, and blocked websites (e.g., *The New York Times*).[17] When pressed on this at the joint press conference with President Obama, President Xi made it clear that foreign press should abide by Chinese laws, and it was their failure to do so that had led to their problems.[18] This includes covering events in Hong Kong in ways at odds with Beijing's policies.

President Xi's comments about the foreign press are also consistent with the tenets of *legal warfare* or "lawfare." This entails the use of the law as a weapon, through legal coercion, legal attacks, legal constraints, and other measures, to help achieve political advantage in support of national goals. President Xi's comment about the press thus took the position that it is the

---

[16] Keith Bradsher and Austin Ramzy, "Taiwan Leaders Stresses Support for Hong Kong Protests," *The New York Times*, October 31, 2014, http://www.nytimes.com/2014/11/01/world/asia/taiwan-president-Ma-Ying-jeou-backs-hong-kong-protesters-while-courting-beijing.html.

[17] Sumit Galhotra, "Amid US-China Talks, Tough Words from Xi Jinping for Foreign Press," Committee to Protect Journalists, November 12, 2014, https://www.cpj.org/blog/2014/11/amid-us-china-talks-tough-words-from-xi-jinping-fo.php.

[18] Mark Landler, "Fruitful Visit by Obama Ends with a Lecture From Xi," *The New York Times*, November 12, 2014, http://www.nytimes.com/2014/11/13/world/asia/china-us-xi-jinping-obama-apec.html?_r=0.

adversary (in this case, foreign press organizations and foreign governments) who were acting illegally, while Beijing's actions were consistent with the law.

Similarly, in dealing with the suffrage issue, the PRC stance has been that it is abiding by the terms of the Basic Law of Hong Kong and the Joint Declaration. As the Hong Kong white paper and the NPC statement both emphasized, interpretation of those key documents is vested in the Standing Committee of the National People's Congress. The right of the people of Hong Kong to cast a vote is being assured—as is the NPC's responsibility to determine the slate of candidate. The system is acting perfectly legally—it is the protestors who are acting in defiance of accepted law. This point was reiterated by China's ambassador to the United States, Cui Tiankai:

> "The issue in Hong Kong is not democracy. It's the rule of law, whether people should respect and maintain rule of law, or whether they should try to hurt it," Cui said. "People's normal life and social order is disrupted. This is hurting the rule of law in Hong Kong. Without rule of law, there's no democracy."[19]

Meanwhile, the protestors in Hong Kong have long been operating in the shadow of Chinese *psychological warfare* activities. The omnipresent threat of the People's Liberation Army and People's Armed Police, even if they were never employed, nonetheless influenced the protestors. It is likely no coincidence that they were self-censoring, deliberately limiting their protests both physically and politically. Similarly, Beijing's harassment of protestors, including not only leaders but rank-and-file, is almost certainly a long-term psychological effort to discourage future protests by highlighting the negative consequences of participating in them at any level.

Implications of the Chinese Reaction for the United States

For the United States, the Chinese actions, both direct and indirect, regarding Hong Kong signal that the next several years may be a period of growing tension between Washington and Beijing for several reasons.

In the first place, the Chinese hard-line regarding the protests in Hong Kong, while masked by a non-violent response, indicates that there is little prospect for political liberalization in the Xi administration. Indeed, the harsh message underscoring the "one country" element of the "one country, two systems" formula suggests a senior Chinese leadership that will brook little, if any, dissent or divergence from Party and national unity. Moreover, this lack of interest in pluralism seems to encompass much of the PRC polity; this is a stance that seems to bind together Xi, other senior Chinese leaders, and even large segments of the broader Chinese and Hong Kong populations, which have apparently evinced little or limited sympathy for the protestors.

---

[19] Isaac Stone Fish. "If You Want Rule of Law, Respect Ours," *Foreign Policy*, November 4, 2014, http://www.foreignpolicy.com/articles/2014/11/04/interview_china_ambassador_US_elections_democracy_hong_kong_freedom_snowden_visas.

Even more problematic, the erosion of support in the HKSAR may suggest to Beijing that it does not need to conduct political reform in order to limit protests or deal with domestic instability. The successful resolution of the Hong Kong situation may be used as an argument by many in China for a strategy of patient attrition—and against one of implementing political liberalization.

This, in turn, would call into question the longstanding assumption that a wealthier China will necessarily be one that will adopt political reforms, leading eventually to greater pluralism and democratization. That this series of developments runs directly counter to longstanding Chinese policy, which opposes "westernization" (and "splittism"), only makes their prospects even less likely.[20]

Consequently, the United States needs to undertake a hedging strategy, even as it continues to seek opportunities to cooperate with the PRC. Such a strategy, however, must first recognize the low probability that the PRC will evolve towards a more liberal, pluralistic political system. Indeed, the Chinese focus on political warfare, and the concomitant employment of such instruments as legal warfare and public opinion warfare against its own population, should serve as a caution regarding interactions with Beijing. Negotiations of any sort must be undertaken with the assumption that they are establishing precedents, not for greater trust, but for political warfare exploitation.

While it may be satisfying to announce a new initiative on climate change or military-to-military confidence-building measures, it is troubling that so few details are forthcoming about precise terms and definitions. Who will determine whether China is in compliance with the agreements? Whose statistics will be used? What will be the consequences of failure to comply? American decision-makers cannot assume an implied common understanding, any more than the people of Hong Kong could assume that "universal suffrage" meant that they could choose whom they voted for.

There is special urgency in improving America's posture in the western Pacific in the coming two years. If the fallout from the Hong Kong protests is a revived debate on Taiwan about its future with the mainland, President Xi Jinping may find himself confronted in 2016 with the unfamiliar phenomenon, to him, of tense cross-strait relations. Xi himself was not part of the senior leadership when Chen Shuibian, the last DPP president, was in office. As important, the People's Liberation Army has enjoyed nearly a decade of consistent, double-digit growth in the intervening years, fielding a substantially improved array of weapons, including more dedicated anti-ship ballistic missiles and other anti-access/area denial capabilities. The United States needs to be able to send a clear signal that it remains committed to the peaceful management of the Taiwan Strait situation—which requires a military posture capable of helping to assure that outcome.

---

[20] Deng Xiaoping enunciated his concerns about "westernization" and "splittism" in the wake of Tiananmen. Gilbert Rozman, *Chinese Strategic Thought Toward Asia* (New York: Palgrave-MacMillan, 2012), pp. 31-32. Hu Jintao and other Chinese leaders echoed this in 2007 and 2012. Congressional-Executive Commission on China, *2007 Annual Report* (Washington, DC: U.S. Congress, 2007), http://www.cecc.gov/publications/annual-reports/2007-annual-report, and "China Sees Culture as a Crucial Battleground," CNN, January 5, 2012, http://www.cnn.com/2012/01/05/world/asia/china-western-culture/.

As important, however, the United States must also strengthen its ties to other states in the region, so that Beijing does not operate under the illusion that it can employ political warfare to delay or dilute the American response. This means expanding security ties with longstanding allies such as Japan, South Korea, and the Philippines, and friends such as Singapore, but also improving relations with other states such as Vietnam, Indonesia, and Malaysia. An obvious element here is also the need to help Taiwan improve its military capabilities. The grudging pace of arms sales from the only country in the world, the U.S., with the capability and willingness to sell them, has created a situation where Taipei can no longer assure control over the air and seas around the island. Upgrades of fighters sold in 1992 fall far short of what is sufficient to right that balance. Taiwan needs new fighter aircraft, and some way of correcting a very serious deficiency in underwater warfare assets.

What is going on in Hong Kong today is a problem in its own right, for the people of Hong Kong and their future. It also, however, reveals a great deal about the PRC that confronts the Administration and Congress, and signals some of the challenges to peace and security in the region. For much of its history, the United States has seen the preservation of regional stability and preventing the rise of a regional hegemon as fundamental to its national interests. China's actions in Hong Kong suggest that Beijing is more likely to be a challenger than a partner to these ends.

Dean Cheng, Senior Research Fellow, The Heritage Foundation

Dean Cheng is currently the Senior Research Fellow for Chinese Political and Military Affairs at the Heritage Foundation. He is fluent in Chinese, and uses Chinese language materials regularly in his work.

Prior to joining the Heritage Foundation, he was a senior analyst with the China Studies Division (previously, Project Asia) at CNA from 2001-2009. He specialized on Chinese military issues, with a focus on Chinese military doctrine and Chinese space capabilities.

Before joining CNA, he was a senior analyst with Science Applications International Corporation (SAIC) from 1996-2001. From 1993-1995, he was an analyst with the US Congress' Office of Technology Assessment in the International Security and Space Division, where he studied the Chinese defense industrial complex.

He has written a number of papers and book chapters examining various aspects of Chinese security affairs, including Chinese military doctrine, the military and technological implications of the Chinese space program, and Chinese concepts of "political warfare." Recent publications include:

- "Information Dominance: PLA Views of Information Warfare and Cyberwarfare," in *Chinese Cybersecurity and Cyberdefense,* ed. by Daniel Ventre (Hoboken, NJ: Wiley Publishers, 2014).

- "China's Military Role in Space," *Strategic Studies Quarterly* (VI, #1, Spring 2012)

- "Chinese Lessons from the Gulf Wars," in *Chinese Lessons from Other People's Wars*, ed. by Andrew Scobell, David Lai, and Roy Kamphausen (Carlisle, PA: Strategic Studies Institute, 2011).

- "Chinese Views on Deterrence," *Joint Force Quarterly* (#60, January 2011)

He has testified before Congress, and spoken at the National Space Symposium, the US National Defense University, Harvard, and MIT. He has appeared frequently on CNN International, the BBC, Voice of America, and National Public Radio to comment on Chinese developments, and has been interviewed by the *Financial Times*, *Washington Post*, Phoenix TV (Hong Kong) and *South China Morning Post*, among others, regarding Chinese space and military activities.

Mr. CHABOT. Dr. Richardson, you are recognized for 5 minutes.

STATEMENT OF SOPHIE RICHARDSON, PH.D., CHINA DIRECTOR, HUMAN RIGHTS WATCH

Ms. RICHARDSON. Mr. Chairman, distinguished members of the subcommittee, thanks for inviting me to testify today. I would like to take my 5 minutes not to go into details about what has happened in the last few weeks, but rather to talk about the kinds of recommendations that will protect human rights in and the autonomy of Hong Kong where tensions between police and protesters really have reached a breaking point.

The extraordinary demonstrations by a cross-section of people in Hong Kong are in our view not simply about the composition of Hong Kong's nomination committee. After waiting patiently for years for China to fulfill its promise of democracy, many are angry at Beijing's political overreach and at the Hong Kong Government's growing tendency to marginalize the interests of the majority on issues ranging from education policy to urban planning.

In the broadest sense, the current tensions are local and logical reactions of people who have enjoyed civil liberties and a reasonably responsive government but who now see these freedoms increasingly threatened and who have a very clear sense of how those rights are denied just across the border. In our view, physically removing demonstrators from the streets of Hong Kong will do little to answer their underlying grievances and will arguably serve to exacerbate them.

The most critical and urgent step the central and Hong Kong Governments can take is to revisit the territory's undemocratic electoral arrangements and ensure that the appropriate ones are fashioned, as required by Article 45 of the Basic Law, ''in light of the actual situation,'' where the majority has repeatedly made clear that it favors genuine democracy.

We urge that both take immediate action, including by developing a time-bound and detailed plan to put into practice universal and equal suffrage. Any proposals for methods of nominations should conform to international human rights standards, including those in the ICCPR, which pertains in Hong Kong.

Hong Kong authorities also can and should immediately meet with protest leaders and submit a new report to the central government acknowledging broad support for genuine democracy and asking the National People's Standing Committee to clarify or retract its August 31 decision.

While it is reassuring to see Hong Kong authorities investigate several police officers who were caught on camera viciously beating a protester, that confidence is undermined by repeated incidents of excessive use of force, including in recent days where police have used pepper spray at close range, hit with batons people who were clearly trying to leave protest areas, or tackle and arrest without warning student protest leaders. We urge the establishment of an independent investigative body to look into the now 1,000-plus complaints regarding police conduct.

At a political level, it would be encouraging if the senior leadership in Beijing could accept the idea that people in the mainland and in Hong Kong want democracy and not construe people's demands for that as a threat to national security. At an absolute minimum, Beijing should stop arresting people in the mainland for their peaceful expressions of support to the demonstrators and lift whatever restrictions have been put in place for demonstrators to enter the mainland.

The United States has expressed concern about violence, the right to peaceful assembly, and the rights to vote and to run. American officials have said that they have expressed these concerns directly to the highest levels of the Chinese Government. But much of the commentary, including President Obama's remarks while in Beijing, has been so calibrated as to be convoluted. Other remarks are superficially sensible, calling, for example, that difference between protesters and authorities be resolved through peaceful dialogue, but seem to deny the reality that Hong Kong people's efforts to do just that have been ignored.

The U.S.'s repeated denials that it had had any role in fomenting or sustaining the demonstrations suggests to us that it is more concerned in assuaging Beijing's irrational fears than standing up robustly for democratic rights. It is appropriate to ask why President Obama could be so publicly restrained on the topic of elections and democracy in Hong Kong while he was in Beijing, yet just few days later offer up extensive commentary and support on the same subject in Burma and later from Australia.

One recalls Assistant Secretary of State Victoria Nuland handing out bread to demonstrators in Maidan Square, American Ambassadors observing elections in other parts of Asia, or the U.S. vociferously decrying rollbacks of democratic rights in other parts of the world. Why not in Hong Kong? Such an approach undermines in our view the U.S.-Hong Kong Policy Act, and it enables other governments, which, for better or for worse, take their cues on these issues from the U.S., to remain virtually silent.

Arguably most problematic in our view, it telegraphs to pro-democracy activists in Hong Kong and the mainland that they can likely only count on perfunctory support or recognition from the United States.

So it is encouraging to us to see the reestablishment of a Hong Kong Caucus here in the Congress and the introduction of an updated Hong Kong Policy Act. We believe this to be a very important tool. We believe that increased U.S. Government scrutiny and regular reporting are and should be seen as a positive obligation, an opportunity to identify critical developments and points of leverage in a territory of extraordinary diplomatic, economic, and strategic interest to the United States.

Thank you.

Mr. CHABOT. Thank you very much.

[The prepared statement of Ms. Richardson follows:]

United States House of Representatives Committee on Foreign Affairs

Subcommittee on Asia and the Pacific

"Hong Kong: A Broken Promise?"

Tuesday, December 2, 2014

Written Testimony of Sophie Richardson

China Director for Human Rights Watch

Mr. Chairman, Ranking Member Faleomavaega, and distinguished Members of the subcommittee, thank you for inviting me to testify today. As protestors remain on the streets of Hong Kong, this discussion is timely, and we hope to clarify the critical human rights issues at stake.

It is appropriate to recall that in 1997 the hope was that not only would Hong Kong's autonomy be respected, and the rights to the freedom of assembly, expression, and political participation there would remain intact, but also that these realities might have a positive effect on the mainland. People in Hong Kong have continued to make clear how much they value an independent judiciary, a free press, a meritocratic civil service, and a professional police force. Yet developments of the past year have shown that in fact, the mainland's politics and disdain for rights are having alarming consequences for those realities, a territory of critical importance to the United States and within the region.

Since 1997, Human Rights Watch has expressed concern over erosions of Hong Kong's autonomy, particularly with respect to the independence of the press, increased interference into Hong Kong politics, and a growing role for Beijing's Central Liaison Office in Hong Kong. Consistent with its attitude towards other regions on its periphery from Tibet to Taiwan, President Xi Jinping's government appears to perceive Hong Kong people's greater demands for a fully elected government—one that responds to their concerns and one in which they are entitled to according to law—as an existential threat. Beijing has insisted that the Chief Executive must be someone who passes a political litmus test set by the Chinese Communist Party, has made clear that efforts by people in Hong Kong to press their demands through every possible peaceful avenue will be rejected, and has moved swiftly to crush any expressions of sympathy in the mainland for pro-democracy efforts in Hong Kong.

The extraordinary demonstrations by a cross-section of people in Hong Kong are in turn not simply about the composition of Hong Kong's nomination committee. After waiting patiently for years for China to fulfill its promise to give democracy, many are angry at the central government's overreach, particularly with respect to its decision to retain control over the selection of Hong Kong's leader. Many expressed growing frustration and a sense of marginalization by the Hong Kong government, arguing that it increasingly failed to respond to the interests of the majority on issues ranging from education policy to urban planning. They are also a reaction to threats to key independent institutions in the territory that have helped protect human rights, and to growing unease over whether the Hong Kong government is serving the interests of the Hong Kong people or the central government when it comes to key decisions. In the broadest sense, the current tensions are local and logical reactions of people who have enjoyed civil liberties, an independent judiciary, a free press, and a reasonably responsive government, but who see these freedoms increasingly threatened, and who have some sense of how these rights are denied just across the border.

Beijing's legal obligations with respect to Hong Kong

The 1984 Sino-British Joint Declaration spells out the terms for transfer of Hong Kong from British to Chinese control. That document stipulates that Hong Kong shall have "a high degree of autonomy" in matters other than national defense and foreign policy, while the Basic Law, Hong Kong's functional constitution, states that universal suffrage is the "ultimate aim" for the selection of the chief executive, the top leader, as well as members of the Legislative Council. The Basic Law also provides that the International Covenant on Civil and Political Rights (ICCPR) applies to Hong Kong, and the Covenant's guarantee of universal and equal suffrage means that people not only have the right to vote in elections, but also that they should have the right to stand for elections regardless of their political views. The committee responsible for monitoring the implementation of the ICCPR has also stated that when the law requires a certain threshold of supporters for nomination, "this requirement should be reasonable and not act as a barrier to candidacy."

Hong Kong's Basic Law states that Hong Kong can move towards the goal of universal suffrage by amending the electoral methods in three steps. First, two-thirds of all Legislative Council members have to endorse the amendments. Second, the current chief executive has to agree to it. Lastly, the amendments have to be reported to China's Standing Committee for the National Peoples' Congress (NPCSC) for approval.

The central government, in a series of decisions made since 1997, has backtracked on this obligation to institute universal and equal suffrage. The commitment to allowing electoral reform to be decided by Hong Kong people was first broken on April 6, 2004, when the NPCSC made an "interpretation" of the Basic Law adding a requirement that the chief executive submit a report to Beijing justifying the need for any further democratization. The decision shifted the initiative in proposing electoral reforms to Beijing's hand-picked chief executive, and away from the Legislative Council. In April 2004, directly after this NPCSC decision, the Chief Executive submitted a report that downplayed the need for substantial reform, and the NPCSC quickly followed this with a decision that ruled out universal suffrage for the 2007 selection of the chief executive and the selection of the 2008 Legislative Council.

In 2007, it ruled again that there would not be universal suffrage for the next elections of the chief executive and the Legislative Council in 2012. However, the 2007 decision also said that universal suffrage was "maybe" in store for the next chief executive election and Legislative Council elections in 2017 and 2020, respectively.

Recent developments

As Hong Kong authorities began in late 2013 to prepare for a public consultation on how the 2017 elections should be carried out, Li Fei, a top mainland official and chairman of Beijing's Basic Law Committee, gave a speech stating that Hong Kong's chief executive must be an individual who "loves the country and loves Hong Kong," and that people who "confront the central government" do not meet this criterion. This followed similar pronouncements by Li's predecessor, Qiao Xiaoyang, as well as the director of the Liaison Office of the Chinese Government in Hong Kong, Zhang Xiaoming. Li added that the nomination committee for the chief executive would be restricted to a small selected group of Hong Kong people who will make a "collective" decision on candidates allowed to run in the election. The position countered earlier proposals by prodemocracy groups advocating a process in which all Hong Kong voters would be considered "members" of the nominating committee and candidates securing a specified number of public nominations would get on the ballot.

Over the subsequent months, the Hong Kong government and large parts of the public made their views clear about democracy and about Hong Kong's future. In early June 2014—shortly after the 25th anniversary of the Tiananmen Massacre—the Chinese government issued a "white paper" asserting "overall jurisdiction" over Hong Kong, and that Hong Kong "is limited to the level of autonomy granted by the central leadership." This was widely seen as a violation of the commitment to "one country, two systems" in which Hong Kong would be granted "a high degree of autonomy," except in foreign affairs and defense. While the substance of the "white paper" was not new, and carries no legal weight, its timing and language were seen as abrasive and unnecessary by many in Hong Kong.

In late June 2014, more than 700,000 Hong Kong people—one in five registered voters— participated in an unofficial, non-binding referendum to choose among three proposals for political reform that ensure universal suffrage via the pro-democracy "Occupy Central with Love and Peace" movement. The central government dismissed this effort as illegal and the product of "anti-China forces." In mid-July, Hong Kong Chief Executive (CE) Leung Chun-ying submitted the results of the government's public consultation to the central government, claiming it was "mainstream opinion" that a subsequent CE "love China and love Hong Kong," that the power to nominate CE candidates should remain vested in a committee controlled by Beijing, and that the legislature should not be democratized before the 2017 elections. The results of the public consultation as presented to the central Chinese government were clearly manipulated, and failed to reflect different views articulated by large segments of the population.

Following the report's submission, on August 31, 2014, the NPCSC handed down its decision, which catalyzed the Occupy demonstrations: while it would allow all eligible voters in Hong Kong to cast ballots for the territory's chief executive, it would impose a stringent screening mechanism that effectively bars candidates the central government in Beijing dislikes from nomination for chief executive.

In reaction to the Chinese government's August 31 rejection of open nominations for Hong Kong's chief executive, Occupy Central protest leaders, pan-democrats, and student protest leaders vowed to launch an "era of civil disobedience." Students boycotted classes between September 22 and 26; as that boycott came to a close, a group of students entered Civic Square, in front of the government headquarters in Admiralty, without permission. Police surrounded the students, and arrested and pepper sprayed some of them. The police treatment of the students provoked a large number of people—about 50,000— to congregate around Civic Square on September 27. "Occupy Central" organizers then announced that they were officially launching their planned demonstrations.

On September 28, Hong Kong police declared the protest illegal, and cordoned off the government headquarters grounds. The announcement drew even more protesters, who demanded access to the government headquarters. After an hours long standoff with police, protesters walked out onto a major thoroughfare that separated them from government headquarters. Police responded with pepper spray, batons, and 87 cans of tear gas. Protesters refused to disperse, and by the next morning they had occupied three sites in Hong Kong. For weeks, two of these sites remained occupied by hundreds of protesters, despite repeated police clearances, and assaults by persons opposing the Occupy movement. After police cleared one site in Mongkok on November 26, protesters responded with "fluid occupation" which involves repeatedly "crossing roads" slowly along the stretch of the former occupy sites to temporarily block traffic, as well as a failed escalation on November 30 to block all access to government headquarters in Admiralty.

Human rights concerns

Human Rights Watch has a host of concerns about human rights violations in Hong Kong, both specific to the protests and to larger issues.

On the core issue of electoral arrangements, the Basic Law guarantees the continued application of the International Covenant on Civil and Political Rights to Hong Kong, which in turn guarantees that people shall not only have the right to vote in elections, but also that they should have the right to stand for elections regardless of their political views. While the August 31 NPCSC decision will expand the vote to choose the Chief Executive to all eligible voters, it retains central government control over the nominating committee that will determine who may run as a candidate for chief executive. As recently as October 23, 2014, the UN's Human Rights Committee expressed concern that the proposed nomination process poses "unreasonable restrictions" on the right to run.

The protests themselves have involved a number of human rights violations.

- Mainland and Hong Kong authorities deemed the protests illegal because organizers had not obtained permission under the Public Order Ordinance. Yet this Ordinance is in tension with international law because it imposes significant restrictions on the freedom of assembly without considering the importance of the right to gather to express grievances, and is susceptible to political abuse.
- The Hong Kong police's use of force, including tear gas and pepper spray, against unarmed protestors is of deep concern. While we note as positive Chief Executive Leung's condemnation of violence against protestors on October 4, and the arrest of seven police in late November for their brutal beating on October 16 of a peaceful demonstrator, the October 6 statement by the Chief Executive that authorities would use "all actions necessary" and evidence of further incidents involving excessive use of force by the police have undermined public confidence in the strict adherence of the police to the UN Basic Principles on the Use of Force and Firearms. Human Rights Watch calls on the Hong Kong government to conduct an independent investigation into police conduct during the protests.
- We are similarly deeply concerned about arrests of peaceful protestors at the beginning of the demonstrations in late September, but also during the late November efforts to clear protestors from particular locations, including the arrests of student demonstration leaders Joshua Wong and Lester Shum.
- We are also concerned that protesters appear to be subject to various types of intrusive surveillance by both the Hong Kong and Chinese governments, which apparently have based decisions to arrest protest leaders and bar others from entering China on their online postings and participation in the protests. The sense of pervasive collection and monitoring of participation in public debates and protests have thrown a pall over Hong Kong's robust civil liberties.

Larger implications

The central and Hong Kong government's failures to engage meaningfully with popular demands for greater democracy in the territory—through a formal consultation process, through a civic referendum, through months of peaceful demonstrations—leaves a longtime bastion of respect for rule of law on edge.

Beijing has made its disdain for the views of people in Hong Kong clear through its extraordinary overreach regarding autonomy, electoral arrangements, and a host of other policy issues. And because the Chinese Communist Party cannot countenance the idea that people in China might actually want participatory governance, it has repeatedly dismissed the demonstrations as a product of external, "anti-China forces."

It has also made clear that it will not tolerate any expressions of support in the mainland for the demonstrators in Hong Kong. More than 100 individuals have been detained in the mainland in recent months for doing as little as posting pictures of themselves holding a sign expressing support for Hong Kong people's demand for genuine universal suffrage. Beijing's unwillingness to allow student leaders or those sympathetic to the demonstrations from Hong Kong into the mainland is an utterly anachronistic and counterproductive strategy for dealing with the concerns there.

None of this bodes well for expectations that China will comply with key international legal obligations, come to grips with peaceful dissent, or accept—for Hong Kong, for Tibet, or for Xinjiang—the idea that many successful governments around the world have officials and administrations from regions benefiting from autonomy arrangements with views divergent from those at the national level. It is also an ominous sign for Hong Kong as a critical space for activists and organizations that work on or monitor developments in China. The efforts of nonviolent protestors in Hong Kong has also triggered expressions of concern across the region, prompting reactions from Tokyo, which rarely speaks publicly about human rights concerns in China, and from Taiwan, where voters appear to have been particularly motivated to reject a government arguing for closer ties to Beijing.

US response

The United States has expressed concern about violence against and by demonstrators, about the right to peaceful assembly, and the rights to vote and to run, and officials have said they have expressed these concerns directly to the highest levels of the Chinese government. Some US commentary, such as the initial statement regarding the August 31 NPCSC interpretation, did not accurately characterize the problem, while other remarks are superficially sensible—calling, for example, that differences be addressed through peaceful dialogue—but seem to deny the reality that Hong Kong peoples' efforts to do just that have been ignored. President Obama's comments on Hong Kong while in Beijing were so calibrated as to be convoluted, and he and other US officials have repeated so frequently that the US has had no role in fomenting or sustaining the demonstrations that it seems more concerned in assuaging Beijing's irrational fears than in standing up robustly for democratic rights.

We believe the US' response to be factually accurate but functionally and diplomatically ineffective. It makes the mistake of focusing disproportionately on the reactions of the Chinese government while forgetting to demonstrate solidarity with those on the front lines of a struggle for democracy. It is appropriate to ask why President Obama could be so publicly restrained on the topics of elections and democracy in Beijing yet a few days later offer up extensive commentary and support on the same subject in Burma, and shortly after in Australia. One thinks about visible gestures of solidarity for democracy elsewhere—for example, US Assistant Secretary of State Victoria Nuland handing out bread to demonstrators in Maidan Square, American ambassadors observing elections (or expressing concerns about those elections' shortcomings) in other parts of Asia, or the US vociferously decrying the rollbacks of democratic rights in other parts of the world. Why not Hong Kong?

To be so reticent has three problematic consequences. It undermines the very purpose of the US-Hong Kong Policy Act, and it enables other governments, which for better or for worse take their cues on these issues from the US, to remain virtually silent. Arguably most problematic, it telegraphs to pro-democracy activists in Hong Kong and the mainland that they can likely only count on perfunctory support or recognition from the United States.

Recommendations

Physically removing demonstrators from the streets of Hong Kong will do little to answer their underlying grievances, and arguably will serve to exacerbate them. Already tensions between protesters and police have risen to a breaking point. The most critical and urgent step the central and Hong Kong governments can take is to revisit the territory's undemocratic electoral arrangements and ensure that appropriate ones are fashioned—as required by article 45 of the Basic Law—"in light of the actual situation," where the majority favors genuine democracy. We urge that both take immediate action, including by developing a time-bound and detailed plan, to put into practice universal and equal suffrage. Both should ensure that any proposals for nominations for the 2017 chief executive elections conform to international human rights standards, including those set out in the ICCPR. Any committee established for nominating candidates for the elections should conform to such requirements.

While it is reassuring to a point to see Hong Kong authorities investigate several police officers who were caught on camera viciously beating a protestor, that confidence is undermined by repeated incidents of excessive use of force. In just the past few days police have appeared to use excessive force in arresting student protest leaders Joshua Wong and Lester Shum on November 26 in Mong Kok as they stood by observing police; no warning or peaceful request to surrender to authorities were issued before police tackled them to the ground. In Admiralty and Mong Kok in the past 48 hours police have used pepper spray at close range after tearing off demonstrators' protective goggles, and used batons to hit people who were clearly trying to leave these areas. The authorities should meet with protest leaders, given that the single discussion held in October yielded no results. Hong Kong authorities should submit a new report to the central government acknowledging broad support for genuine democracy and ask the NPCSC to clarify or retract its August 31 decision to make the nomination committee for the chief executive genuinely "broadly representative," as articulated in the Basic Law. The Hong Kong authorities should also take steps to further democratize the semi-democratic Legislative Council.

The central government in Beijing should realize Hong Kong's political system is unsustainable and must be fixed to make it more responsive to people in the territory. Each of the chief executives handpicked by Beijing has proven deeply unpopular with significant numbers of people in Hong Kong. At the political level, it would be encouraging if the senior leadership in Beijing could accept the idea that people in the mainland and Hong Kong want democracy, and not construe Hong Kong peoples' demands for democracy as a threat to national security. At a minimum, Beijing should stop arresting people in the mainland for peaceful expressions of support to the demonstrators, and lift whatever restrictions have been put in place so that demonstrators can enter the mainland.

It is encouraging to see the reestablishment of a Hong Kong caucus here in the Congress, and the introduction of an updated Hong Kong Policy Act. We believe that increased US government scrutiny and regular reporting are and should be seen as a positive obligation—an opportunity to identify critical developments and points of leverage in a territory of considerable diplomatic, economic, and strategic interest to the United States. Equally important, we urge the US to be consistent in its support to democratic movements around the world. The people of Hong Kong deserve no less than their counterparts in other countries.

Mr. CHABOT. Ms. Currie, you are recognized for 5 minutes.

STATEMENT OF MS. KELLEY CURRIE, SENIOR FELLOW, PROJECT 2049 INSTITUTE

Ms. CURRIE. Thank you, Mr. Chairman. And thank you to the members of the committee, in particular Mr. Faleomavaega.

It is an honor to be here on your last hearing and have the opportunity to speak on this subject. It is a real challenge, however, to follow my two colleagues who have so ably covered so many of the issues here. I will try to add something with my remarks.

I have got a written testimony that I would like to submit for the record.

Mr. CHABOT. Without objection, so ordered.

Ms. CURRIE. When Mr. Salmon talked about traveling to Hong Kong in 1997, he traveled with my former boss, John Porter, on that trip. My involvement in Hong Kong began with working for Mr. Porter for 5 years in the early and mid-1990s—and late 1990s too, I guess—and his leadership on that issue inspired me to continue to follow the events in Hong Kong and inspired my respect for the people of Hong Kong and the efforts that they have made over the past 30 years since the signing of the Joint Declaration to preserve their democratic rights and freedoms.

And watching what has happened over the past 2 months and indeed in recent years, as Beijing has carefully tried to rachet back the democratic prerogatives and freedoms of the Hong Kong people, has been a very frustrating act. When I worked in the Congress— and Mr. Rohrabacher, Mr. Salmon, and others will remember these days—the Congress was quite active on Hong Kong issues and took a leading role in pushing the administration forward in defending the rights and prerogatives of Hong Kong people.

Unfortunately, in recent years both the Congress and the administration have gone relatively silent on Hong Kong. In particular, as the situation has evolved, we have not seen the kind of activism that marked those years around the handover. That is natural because that was a particularly important time. But the times now have shown that we need to maintain a focus on what is going on in Hong Kong and continue to follow up on the promises that the United States made when it took up the mantle as Hong Kong's guarantor in 1997 as the British retreated.

I believe that this is a role that the United States took up willingly and because it has interests in Hong Kong, as Mr. Cheng as so ably outlined. But it also is aligned with our values. And that is why it is so disappointing to see how the U.S. has not stood up for the values of the Hong Kong people as well.

I would like to just go to follow up on some of the recommendations that Sophie has mentioned about how the Congress can be more active.

The U.S. handling of Hong Kong has hardly been the only example where our reticence has encouraged the worst impulses of the Chinese regime. Our Hong Kong policy approach takes place against a broader backdrop of reluctance to publicly call Beijing out over abuses that are rooted in the structural authoritarian nature of the regime.

Beginning with the period leading up to the 2008 Olympics, there has been a perceptible change in U.S. willingness to publicly, consistently, and vigorously stand up for the rights of Chinese dissidents, Tibetans, Uighurs, and other persecuted groups. All democratic governments have become more reluctant to speak out over this period, but the absence of a strong U.S. voice has exacerbated this long-term trend.

Given the strong message that the people of Hong Kong have sent the world through the Umbrella Movement, however, it is clear that the U.S. needs to start acting both on its values and its interests in Hong Kong in a more forceful way. The recent efforts to again require annual reports on Hong Kong are a good start. But Congress needs to hold the administration accountable for making these reports a serious policy effort, not just a useless box-checking exercise, which they had become toward the end when they ended after 2007. I don't know if you have read the old reports recently, but they are almost content-free, and they virtually ignore what was happening on the ground in Hong Kong, both in terms of the democracy movement that was emerging there and the growth of civil society and the role that Beijing was playing.

I believe that in order to achieve a more meaningful report, the Hong Kong Policy Act should be amended so that the next review or the next report the executive branch is required to conduct a full interagency review pursuant to the presidential determination authority in Section 202 that relates to Hong Kong's autonomous status and whether it continues to be preserved and include detailed findings regarding whether Hong Kong is sufficiently autonomous to continue receiving the beneficial treatments that it currently receives.

In addition to findings on detailed issues in cooperation with counterparts in Hong Kong, the report should also focus on the overall political context and progress for its genuine democratic reforms. The House Foreign Affairs and Senate Foreign Relations Committees should consider holding annual joint hearings on the reports as well. And Congress should also speak out more directly on its concerns through passing of resolutions and legislative action as needed.

The administration also needs to speak up in defense the Hong Kong more publicly, more often, and more clearly. It should stop issuing the kind of confused statements that Dr. Richardson mentioned and that ignore China's failure to live up to the promise of ''One Country, Two Systems''. We should also not forget those on the mainland who were detained solely for expressing support for the Umbrella Movement.

The U.S. should work with his partners in the U.K. To address China's implementation of the Joint Declaration through efforts such as joint commissions of inquiry and joint demarches. The U.K. Is our closest ally and international partner, and their credibility is on the line here as well, due to their failure to stand up for liberal values in Hong Kong.

Likewise, we should look for opportunities where they may exist at the U.N., bearing in mind the low likelihood of any effective action. However, Beijing deeply dislikes being confronted at the U.N., so those opportunities at least do put the issues in a forum where they have to respond to them.

The U.S., the U.K., and Commonwealth countries such as Canada and Australia, should also develop a joint protocol and treatment of student visa applicants who have been arrested for peaceful political activity. This is a very important issue because of the importance of education and study abroad for Hong Kong students and our requirement that if you have been arrested you have to list this on your visa application. We shouldn't penalize people for engaging in civic activity in Hong Kong.

Mr. CHABOT. Is your testimony about done?

Ms. CURRIE. Yes. I am done.

Mr. CHABOT. Thank you.

Ms. CURRIE. Finally, any cuts in Cantonese broadcasting on RFA and VOA should be restored so that we can continue to get a positive message out as media censorship rachets up in Hong Kong and outlets for genuine expression continue to be closed down there. Thank you.

Mr. CHABOT. Thank you.

[The prepared statement of Ms. Currie follows:]

Written Testimony of Kelley E. Currie
Senior Fellow, Project 2049 Institute
As Submitted to the House Committee on Foreign Affairs'
Subcommittee on Asia and the Pacific Hearing on

"Hong Kong: A Broken Promise?"

December 2, 2014

Chairman Chabot, Ranking Member Faleomavaega, and Members of the Committee,

Thank you for holding this hearing on the subject of Hong Kong's democratic future and the implementation of China's promises to provide Hong Kong with a high degree of autonomy. I am honored to join this panel with my colleagues from Human Rights Watch and the Heritage Foundation, two institutions that have long been at the vanguard of the fight for human rights and freedom in Hong Kong. My testimony today will focus on issues related to the legal and policy framework for US engagement on Hong Kong, and how the US government should respond to the current challenge to Hong Kong's democratic development.

This hearing comes as the Hong Kong authorities have moved forcefully against the peaceful pro-democracy demonstrators of the so-called Umbrella Movement, who have spent the past two months demanding that China allow Hong Kong's people the genuine right to choose their own leaders. The demonstrators – led by students and young people who have shown incredible civic spirit, determination and courage -- have been calling for a review of China's August 2014 diktat that Beijing must approve the selection of candidates for Chief Executive when the Hong Kong people take their first direct vote for that position in elections scheduled for 2017. The arrest of the most well-known student leaders over the weekend is particularly troubling, as it signals that Chinese and Hong Kong authorities are no longer interested in trying to resolve this stand-off through dialogue, but rather are determined to crush legitimate expressions of popular dissent through plain coercion.

While such an outcome would be a foregone conclusion in any other Chinese city, one could be excused for hoping the resolution could be different in Hong Kong due to its unique status of being governed not just by China's whim, but also by international agreements that assured its way of life and freedoms would be protected under authoritarian Chinese rule. Beijing agreed in the 1984 Sino-British Joint Declaration to maintain Hong Kong's 'way of life' and by 1997, that way of life included an expectation of democratic rights and accountable governance. Beijing made it clear early on that they were not happy with what it perceived as last-ditch efforts by the departing British to place Hong Kong on a democratic trajectory. Nonetheless, they usually tried to make a virtue of this situation by arguing that

Hong Kong under Chinese rule would experience greater democracy and human rights than the British had ever allowed. And they were right, up to a point.

Unfortunately, since the signing of the Joint Declaration in 1984, Beijing's authoritarian tendencies have repeatedly won out. Over the past thirty years, Chinese leaders' mania for control and innate distrust of democracy has led them to waste multiple opportunities to get 99% of what they wanted without enduring the kinds of protests that have rocked Hong Kong for the past two months and periodically since 1997. In this latest confrontation, as in the past, the Chinese authorities refused to negotiate in good faith with and attempted to discredit moderate democrats such as Martin Lee and Anson Chan, who sought to reach an accommodation on the issues surrounding implementation of universal suffrage and other ambiguities of Hong Kong's mini-constitution, the Basic Law. Instead, the Chinese authorities issued a National People's Congress Standing Committee decision that put Beijing firmly in control of who Hong Kongers could vote for in the Chief Executive election. By rejecting any compromise with moderate democrats in favor of confrontation with less established forces, Beijing is falling back on its old Marxist playbook and sowing the seeds of long-term discontent in Hong Kong, much as it has on the mainland.

In the same vein, the BBC reported on November 30, that the Chinese ambassador to the UK told the chair of a British parliamentary committee charged with investigating the implementation of the 1984 Sino-British Joint Declaration that its members would not be permitted to enter Hong Kong on their fact finding mission. Sir Richard Ottaway, chairman of the House of Commons Foreign Affairs Committee, had previously been warned by Chinese authorities that the MPs trip would represent an "unwelcome interference into the affairs of another country" and a show of support for the "illegal activity" of pro-democracy protesters.

Beijing has long relied on a mantra of 'non-interference in internal affairs' to combat other countries' allegations of human rights abuses, but there is a breathtaking quality to China telling the British – the other party in the international treaty that guarantees Hong Kong's "one country, two systems" arrangement – to mind their own business. It is almost as incredible as assertions that the people of Hong Kong are not ready for democracy. Prime Minister David Cameron has responded with tougher rhetoric in defense of the UK's interests and Hong Kong's rights, but after several years of acquiescing to Chinese bullying in the name of preserving or restoring commercial and diplomatic ties, the UK's protests are easily ignored.

Both by default and because of our own enduring interests there, the United States remains the key guarantor of Hong Kong's freedoms, as it has since 1997. But we too have lost our voice over the years. When Congress passed the Hong Kong Policy Act in 1992, the US declared that:

> *The human rights of the people of Hong Kong are of great importance to the United States and are directly relevant to United States interests in Hong Kong. A fully successful transition in the exercise of sovereignty*

over Hong Kong must safeguard human rights in and of themselves.
Human rights also serve as a basis for Hong Kong's continued economic
prosperity.

At the time the Act was passed, Members and Senators often expressed their hope that post-reversion "Hong Kong would change China more than China would change Hong Kong." And Beijing was already accusing the US of 'interfering in its internal affairs' with the Act, and China's hand-picked incoming Chief Executive Tung Chee-wah attacked Democratic Party Chairman Martin Lee as unpatriotic for supporting it. The US Congress did not let these accusations intimidate it away from continuing to press for Hong Kong's rights and freedoms, and continued passing resolutions, holding hearings, writing letters and directly engaging Chinese authorities on their concerns.

However, when Congress and the administration have gone silent on Hong Kong, the Chinese have pushed their advantage. The US response to negative political developments in Hong Kong has generally been muted since 1997. In 2007, Wu Bangguo, the chairman of the National People's Congress Standing Committee, confirmed Beijing's true intentions when he chillingly intoned that, "Hong Kong had considerable autonomy only because the central government had chosen to authorize that autonomy." That tenth anniversary of the handover also was the year the US stopped issuing annual reports on Hong Kong. But even before the State Department stopped producing the report, they had long become box-checking exercises that scarcely commented on either the growing organic democratic movement in Hong Kong or the related local discontent with the creeping authoritarianism of Beijing's rule.

US handling of Hong Kong has hardly been the only example where our reticence has encouraged the worst impulses of the Chinese regime. Our Hong Kong policy approach takes place against a backdrop of broader reluctance to publicly call Beijing out over abuses that are rooted in the structural authoritarian nature of its regime. Beginning with the period leading up to the 2008 Beijing Olympics, there has been a perceptible change in US willingness to publicly, consistently and vigorously stand up for rights of Chinese dissidents, Tibetans, Uighurs and other persecuted groups. All democratic governments have become more reluctant to speak out over this period, but the absence of a strong US voice has exacerbated this long-term trend.

Given the strong message that the Hong Kong people have sent the world through the Umbrella Movement, however, it is clear the US needs to start acting on both its interests and values in Hong Kong in a more forceful way.

- Recent efforts to again require annual reports on Hong Kong are a good start but Congress needs to hold the administration accountable for making them a serious policy effort, rather than a useless box-checking exercise. In order to achieve this the Hong Kong Policy Act should be amended so that as part of the next report, the executive branch will conduct a full inter-agency review pursuant to the presidential determination authority in Sec. 202 and include detailed findings regarding whether Hong Kong remains "sufficiently autonomous" to continue receiving the beneficial treatments that currently extend to it. In addition to findings related to various cabinet and sub-cabinet level agencies and their cooperation with their counterparts in Hong Kong, the report should also focus on the overall political context and progress toward genuine democratic reforms. While such a comprehensive review would be impractical on an annual basis, the "determination" section of the report would be updated annually and fully examined on a multi-year basis as directed by Congress.

- House Foreign Affairs and Senate Foreign Relations Committees should consider holding annual joint hearings on the reports as well, complete with high-level administration officials who are publicly called to account for US efforts on behalf of Hong Kong and witnesses who can speak directly on behalf of the Hong Kong people. Congress can also speak directly on its concerns through passing of non-binding resolutions.

- The administration also needs to speak up in defense of Hong Kong, more publicly, more often and more clearly. It should stop issuing confused statements that ignore China's failure to live up to the promise of 'one country, two systems', and paper over the denial of universal suffrage represented by Beijing's current approach. We also should not forget those on the mainland who were detained solely for expressing support for the Umbrella Movement.

- The US should work with the UK to address China's implementation of the Joint Declaration through joint commissions of inquiry and joint demarches. The UK is our closest ally and international partner, and their credibility has taken a severe hit due to their failure to stand up for liberal values in Hong Kong. Likewise, we should look for opportunities in UN venues to work with like-minded countries to raise our concerns. While the likelihood of effective UN action is low, Beijing deeply dislikes having to defend its behavior in such forums.

- The US, the UK and commonwealth countries such as Canada and Australia, should develop a joint protocol on treatment of students visa applicants who were arrested for peaceful political activity. Their civic activism should not serve as a barrier to their attending universities in the US and other democratic countries. Joint maintenance of a database of 'known' students and shared practices in handling their applications would be the most effective approach, and could be handled through a negotiated MOU.

- Finally, past cuts and elimination of Cantonese broadcasts on RFA and VOA should be reversed to the extent possible, even if this just means making available rebroadcasts of old programming, or making creative use of user-generated content that would monitored for topicality and appropriateness.

For most of the past 30 years, Chinese authorities generally have sought to reassure the international community in general and the US in particular that Hong Kong would retain its special character under Chinese rule. After the signing of the Joint Declaration in 1984, UK, Hong Kong and Chinese authorities undertook a major effort to convince skeptics in the US Congress and elsewhere that Hong Kong's reversion to Chinese sovereignty would not mean the imposition of Chinese-style authoritarianism or socialism. At that time, Beijing was eager to have high-level, official delegations attend the 1997 handover ceremony, and consistently sought to downplay the control it would have over Hong Kong's internal governance. Chinese interlocutors constantly assured US officials that Beijing would do nothing to 'kill the goose that lays the golden eggs.'

However, there were always signs that China's authoritarian character was not flexible enough to permit the 'one country, two systems' framework to flourish, and we have never paid enough attention to those signs. While the worst-case scenarios have not happened, it is clear that China has undermined the institutions that are necessary for democratic development and taken a broadly paternalistic approach to Hong Kong's governance that is at odds with the cosmopolitan and sophisticated character of the city and its people. At the same time, China itself has retrenched authoritarianism at home and broadly cracked down on dissent in a way that further undermines confidence in its rule over Hong Kong.

Our failure to object strenuously over the past 14 years since the handover has not caused Beijing to give in to its authoritarian tendencies, but we have certainly enabled this outcome. The brave students of the Umbrella Movement have given us a chance to change our approach, and stand with the people of Hong Kong. While external calls for genuine universal suffrage and respect for the rights of Hong Kongers won't fundamentally alter the regime's mindset, they may help to change their short-term calculus on how it handles the current situation. And when Chinese officials tell US officials that Hong Kong is not their concern, we must firmly disagree. Then we can tell them they are free to ignore our demarches but that sooner or later they will have listen to the voices of their own citizens, in Hong Kong and beyond.

Thank you and I look forward to your questions.

###

Mr. CHABOT. And we thank all the witnesses for the testimony. I will now recognize myself for 5 minutes.

It is disconcerting to know that while protests in Hong Kong continued, the administration was working behind the scenes to finalize deals and new initiatives with China which were announced following the APEC Summit last month, deals that raise a lot of questions themselves. I think it is logical to conclude that one of the reasons for the administration's weak responses and tepid support for pro-democracy forces in Hong Kong was to ensure that these deals didn't fall through.

Looking ahead, what are the potential tradeoffs for U.S. policymakers between more forcefully pursuing democratic reform in Hong Kong on one hand versus pursuing other goals with Beijing? Do you think the administration's tip-toeing on providing support for the people of Hong Kong is ultimately more harmful for our role in Asia than helpful?

And I would welcome any of the panel members. Dr. Cheng, would you like to take that?

Mr. CHENG. Well, sir, to begin with, I think that one of the great flaws of the approach that you have outlined that the administration is pursuing is the fact that many of these agreements, at least at this point, have few published details. And the devil, as they say, is in the details, especially because the Chinese have demonstrated with the issue of suffrage their adeptness at legal warfare.

So with the example of the climate change regulations, who will measure China's emissions? Whose statistics will they use? We know that Chinese statistics are often only perhaps glancingly associated with reality. As a result, we seem to be placing ourselves at the, essentially, mercy of Chinese statistics. To trade off our longstanding commitment on the issue of values, as my fellow witnesses have highlighted, in exchange for a promise of Chinese compliance based on their statistics makes buying a pig in a poke a sure guaranteed bargain by comparison.

At the same time, it raises questions among many of our allies about the kind of allied and commitment we have to them. If we are not going to stand up for our principles, things of longstanding interest, in exchange for airy promises, what happens when it is the potential commitment of U.S. force, whether it is to places like the Senkakus or to ensuring freedom of the seas in the South China Sea?

Mr. CHABOT. Let me ask a different question to the other two witnesses if I can here, because my time, I am through it already.

This past weekend, the most well-known student leaders were arrested, including Joshua Wong and Lester Shum, in a manner that demonstrated an alarming level of force from the Hong Kong police. Ms. Richardson or Ms. Currie, do either of you have an update on the status of these individuals or do you have a sense of whether they will be charged, and if so what they might be charged with?

Ms. RICHARDSON. Thanks for the question. The footage of their detention was indeed alarming. There appears to have been no provocation. They did not seem to be presenting any sort of imminent threat to the police. They are also hardly, if they were standing right here, I think we could say that they are not especially physically threatening people. And so the way in which they were arrested that day is particularly alarming. They were tackled to the ground, they were cuffed, no warning was given, and no request seems to have been issued that they effectively surrender themselves.

They have both been released. It is not clear whether charges are going to be pursued. It is worth nothing that Mr. Wong was actually previously detained for about 48 hours until a judge, in really the finest we expect of Hong Kong's judges, essentially said the police have absolutely no basis to have detained him and let him go. But that was not until he had been detained and his computer had been seized and searched.

It is hard not to see tactics like this as both evidence of lack of discipline in some circumstances on the part of the police, but also a way of telegraphing to other student leaders that this is what might be in store for them as well.

Mr. CHABOT. Thank you.

Let me squeeze one last question here and a quick response, if I can. Today the founders of the pro-democracy campaign asked student protesters to retreat over concerns of growing violence at the hands of the police, who have used batons and pepper spray and teargas to drive back crowds.

If they do indeed back down and return home, where do we go from here? Will that essentially indicate that they are capitulating to China or, as the founders stated, is it rather a silent denunciation of a heartless government?

Ms. CURRIE. I am going to go with the latter. I think that what has been amazing, not just the past 2 months but Scholarism and the Occupy Hong Kong With Love and Peace movements that predate the past 2 months. And the activities that they have undertaken have shown a level of civic commitment, discipline, and just plain politeness and competence in engaging the authorities, I think that many people have been surprised by the youth of Hong Kong and heartened by how they have stepped forward and filled in this space.

I think that Beijing fell back on its usual Marxist-Leninist tactics of ignoring the moderate opposition of Martin Lee, Emily Lau, Anson Chans of Hong Kong who wanted to engage them through official channels and do things moderately. And that didn't create enough of a crisis in order to justify heavyhanded rule, so they had to force a confrontation. But, unfortunately for Beijing, the demonstrators and the people involved in the Umbrella Movement have shown themselves to be of the highest caliber of character for the most part, with a few exceptions, obviously, but when you have that many people involved there will be.

But I don't think they are going anywhere. The ideals they represent and the voices they represent and the issues that they represent aren't going anywhere, so they aren't either.

Mr. CHABOT. Thank you. My time has expired. Let me just conclude by saying very briefly that I am very heartened by the people of Hong Kong and the bravery and the standing up for their rights that we have seen. I have to say I am disheartened by the administration's lack of support there, just as I was in the Green Revolution in Iran a few years back.

And my time has expired. I will now yield to the ranking member for his questions.

Mr. FALEOMAVAEGA. Thank you, Mr. Chairman.

I certainly want to thank all our three witnesses this afternoon for their statements and the positions they have taken concerning this important issue.

Just wanted to ask all the three members of panel, the administration supposedly says that they do not take a position at this time toward the situation now in Hong Kong. Do you support universal suffrage or do the protesters there in Hong Kong, what is your perception? If I were Chinese, I would say this is a local matter, what is it there for Americans to tell me what to do and how to do it? And I would like to ask the three panelists for your response to that.

Ms. CURRIE. There are internationally recognized standards for what universal suffrage is. And it includes, as one of the members earlier referred to, one person, one vote. And it also includes the right of people to choose their own leaders.

This is very important. In Burma, President Obama talked about this in the context of the Burmese elections, about the need for the Burmese people to be able to choose their own leaders. But yet in the Hong Kong context the administration says we don't take sides. This is deeply problematic.

Mr. FALEOMAVAEGA. Dr. Richardson.

Ms. RICHARDSON. Just another point about international law, which is equally unbelievably clear that people have the right to run. There cannot be restrictions, undue restrictions on who is able to run, which is really the crux of the August 31 decision.

I think people in Hong Kong have made it painfully clear that they want to be able to vote, they want to be able to choose who they are voting for and how these people represent them. I think this is really not just about the finer points of electoral arrangements. I think people feel that the Hong Kong Government progressively less responsive to them and that this is another way in which their ability to control or have input into public policy is eroding.

But I think the important point is that they have made it clear what they want. Also, look, let's just be very clear, the administration is perfectly capable of taking sides either in choosing party A or party B when it suits it. It is also perfectly capable of answering this question with respect to principle, and it has been awfully squeamish in both regards.

Mr. FALEOMAVAEGA. Mr. Cheng.

Mr. CHENG. I would also just note here that the National People's Congress's white paper in June and its statement on August 31 would seem to constitute at best an infringement, if not a violation in many ways of both the Joint Declaration and the Basic Law. Now, it is up to the National People's Congress to interpret these aspects, but to come up with an interpretation that is almost directly 180 degrees from what is stated really calls into question China's commitment to upholding international agreements.

So the issue here is as much one of do you live up to your international commitments, and, if you don't, then it is for the United States, a key trade partner, a key presumably negotiating partner, to call you on this as part of enforcing international order.

Mr. FALEOMAVAEGA. So will there be an agreement among the three members of the panel that there should be universal freedom to that extent, allowing the people of Hong Kong to decide for themselves their future politically and economically? Does that seem to be your position on this?

Mr. CHABOT. I think all three witnesses have nodded in the affirmative.

Mr. FALEOMAVAEGA. I have said in my statement that I have always been very critical of our U.S. foreign policy toward the Asia-Pacific region, which has been no policy, in my opinion. I take this position because I feel that the mentality and the focus of our entire foreign policy is toward the Middle East and Europe, but when it comes to Asia-Pacific we get mixed signals. Every administration, every Congress, if you will, and even the people and the leaders in the Asia-Pacific region that I have met, they say, hey, what is going on? What is your position? Give me these basic principles that we are discussing.

So that is my concern, Mr. Chairman.

And would you like to comment on that?

Ms. RICHARDSON. I would love to comment on that and bring it back to a point that Mr. Rohrabacher raised in his opening remarks about, you were, I think, referencing a piece that was in Foreign Policy about whether the Obama administration has any senior people on China. I mean, look, the administration is filled with lots of people who have lots of China experience. Some of them are ferocious defenders of human rights, and we appreciate them.

I think the problem is that there is no policy, and there hasn't been for quite some time. And arguably one of our real points of frustration has been to be presented with significant numbers of people with fairly deep China experience who have yet to craft a policy that is coordinated and executed from senior levels on down.

Mr. FALEOMAVAEGA. I am sorry. My time is up. Thank you, Mr. Chairman.

Mr. CHABOT. Thank you very much.

The gentleman from Pennsylvania is recognized for 5 minutes.

Mr. PERRY. Thank you, Mr. Chairman.

Ladies and gentlemen, I will start with Dr. Richardson and Ms. Currie. Recently Secretary Earnest made the statement the United States supports universal suffrage in Hong Kong in accordance with Basic Law, and we support the aspirations of the Hong Kong people, while at the same time—I think you already alluded to this. I just feel like it is important to have it on the record—the U.S. Consulate in Hong Kong said, we do not take sides in the discussion of Hong Kong's political development.

With that, is the administration sending mixed signals in Hong Kong or to Hong Kong to the protestors? Same thing, are they sending mixed signals to Beijing? And is there a clear policy at all from the administration in this regard?

Ms. CURRIE. Yes, they are sending mixed signals, both to the protestors and to Beijing. And, no, there is not a clear policy. I think that what you saw was the consulate issue a terrible statement that they were called on the carpet for, rightly so, by various quarters, and then Josh Earnest, trying to walk it back into something that is a little more appropriate, in line with the historic posture of the United States on Hong Kong and the Hong Kong Policy Act.

But, again, it fits a pattern that Sophie just described of incoherence, of reactiveness. You have the so-called pivot or the rebalance that is unbalanced and not strategic in any real way and not rooted in American principles in any real way, and it causes them to constantly be spinning around saying one thing one day and something else the next. It is a problem across the board.

Mr. PERRY. Okay. I just wanted to get your input because I see this as a continued failure of foreign policy of which there are many strikes at this point. But moving on, other than the rhetoric that Mr. Sherman talked about earlier that we can engage in, I want to see us take more concrete action, or some concrete action.

And let me just ask you this. Regarding what the Congress should do, United States Congress should do, would passing legislation to make Hong Kong eligible for the U.S. visa waiver program be a viable alternative that might make some form of a difference.

Ms. RICHARDSON. It strikes me as a perfectly sensible strategy to pursue. I think one of the difficulties in developing legislative responses to the crisis in Hong Kong is ensuring that the people of Hong Kong aren't being punished for essentially the mistakes or the problems caused by the central government or the failures of the Hong Kong authorities. It is difficult sometimes to separate those out.

I do want to go back very briefly to the question you asked a moment ago which is simply to say that I think when this administration has been good on China and human rights issues, it has been very good. I will point, for example, to its reactions to the life sentence given to Ilham Tohti, a very prominent Uighur economist. There were statements from the White House, from the State Department, from the Secretary. The President mentioned Ilham Tohti at a speech in New York. But the unwillingness to deal with these issues or raise them publicly while in Beijing or, indeed, give remarks to the Chinese press in an interview to Xinhua, I think really undermines the comments about Ilham Tohti.

The President made reference to ETIM, the East Turkestan independence movement. Experts have debated for years about whether it even exists, without providing information to substantiate that claim and in effect hang a bulls eye on any Uighur identified by the Chinese Government as being associated with ETIM is hugely problematic. And so it is this very, very inconsistent response. And one would like to think that this far in you could get a more consistent reaction, but that seems to be extremely difficult.

Mr. PERRY. Because my time is going to expire and I want to spend some time with Mr. Cheng, I think I will stick around for round two. But just keeping with your current line of thinking and responding, do you think that what you just described as putting a bulls eye, so to speak, on those folks that would be interested in that movement, is that borne out of ignorance? Is there some method to it from this administration or are they just clueless about it? I mean, how does that come about? They have not consulted with the right people that know something about the situation?

Ms. RICHARDSON. Mr. Perry, I would be delighted to have a good answer to that question. I don't.

Let me be very clear. There have been horrific attacks against civilians in Xinjiang. That is absolutely clear, and we have condemned them. But I think the administration has fallen peculiarly prey to a Chinese Government line. We are going to hear that line again and again and again from Beijing in every discussion about Xinjiang and terrorism for years to come. How that sentence wound up in that interview, I do not know. And believe me, it is not for want of asking.

Mr. PERRY. Thanks, Mr. Chairman. I yield back.

Mr. CHABOT. Thank you. The gentleman's time has expired.

The gentleman from California, Mr. Sherman, is recognized.

Mr. SHERMAN. I want to pick up where the gentleman from Pennsylvania left off. I can't agree with the idea of a visa waiver for either Hong Kong or China, simply because we can't create a circumstance where anybody who can get a Hong Kong passport gets right into the United States. Over half the illegal immigrants or roughly half the illegal immigrants in the United States today came here on an airplane and their entry into the United States was legal. And given the incredible poverty of some in China, and even some in Hong Kong, I don't know if we can go visa waiver. I do see the reciprocity approach of how long a visa, once issued, is good for and how many different trips you can make, but those are only to people that we have decided will not be economic immigrants to the United States.

But I do want to pick up on the gentleman from Pennsylvania's question, and that is, other than rhetoric is there anything we can do to express our dissatisfaction with this violation of the commitments of Beijing to the people of Hong Kong?

Mr. CHENG. Well, to begin with, sir, on the issue of visas, for example, one of the things that clearly is important here is the opportunity to bring more information from Hong Kong out to the broader world and more information from the outside world to Hong Kong. Part of the issue here is the fact that the Chinese refuse to issue visas to journalists, and in fact at the joint press conference between President Obama and President Xi, he in turn lectured the New York Times about how if you don't get visas, it is your own fault.

Mr. SHERMAN. Right. And that applies even to journalists going to Hong Kong, let alone those going to the rest of China.

Mr. CHENG. Certainly there are controls, observations and the rest.

Mr. SHERMAN. I think we have gotten an awful lot of information from Hong Kong during the present unrest. It is not like there is a shortage of Americans visiting Hong Kong. I think we are getting a fair amount of information.

Mr. CHENG. We are, but that information comes out. That information doesn't necessarily go back in, and the Chinese are very, very tightly controlling their media. At a minimum, demanding reciprocity, given the number of official Chinese journalists in the United States, and creating that kind of reciprocity on the press visa aspect, would be——

Mr. SHERMAN. I certainly don't want to reduce the number of Chinese journalists here.

Ms. Currie, I think you had a important point also about visas, which is that being arrested by the Chinese Government for a political crime should not count against somebody in getting a visa to the United States. Does the State Department have the procedures now to make sure that we can tell the difference between a pickpocket and a political activist.

Ms. CURRIE. Frankly, we don't really, especially in a high-volume visa office like the consular office in Hong Kong.

Mr. SHERMAN. Do we even have something on the form where you can say, I have been arrested but it was political?

Ms. CURRIE. There is a place on the form where you say that you were arrested, and then you can explain the circumstances. But the average consular officer, you have to remember, is a brand new foreign service officer usually serving their first tour overseas, and their inclination is generally to say no.

Mr. SHERMAN. We have got to somehow bring in the State Department, and I don't care how junior these people are, they can't be discriminating against people because they have been arrested for political rights and expressing themselves politically.

I just want to say that this all comes from our insane trade policy toward China since we granted MFN. We have this enormous trade deficit which creates this huge debt which causes Americans to shrink from criticizing China, because oh, my God, they loan us so much money, money we wouldn't have to borrow if we were allowed to sell our goods to China. And it also creates these enormous profits that create some of the biggest names in our country, biggest corporations in our country, becoming lobbyists against doing anything to undermine the insane trade policy that started it all.

I don't think we are going to have a balanced policy toward Hong Kong until we have balanced trade. I might also point out that if we had balanced trade with China we would have a labor shortage and significantly increased wages in this country. That could happen if we adopted Warren Buffett's idea of legally required balanced trade. I don't think that is likely to be adopted any time soon. I don't know whether Mr. Cheng had a comment on that.

Mr. CHENG. Sir, I think that part of the fundamental concept of trade is, of course, competitive advantage. Whatever else the Chinese are guilty of, and they are guilty of quite a few things, the reality is that we are not going to create or recreate the textile industry in this country regardless of——

Mr. SHERMAN. Sir, reclaiming my time. Germany exports to China. We don't. Those are political decisions. The American workers are the best in the world. The American products are best in the world. And the huge trade deficit is not because we don't provide value. It is because of the slanted trade policies and IP policies of China. And blaming the American worker, blaming the American product for the decisions made in Beijing is not the way I want to go.

I yield back.

Mr. CHABOT. The gentleman's time has expired.

The gentleman from California, Mr. Rohrabacher, is recognized.

Mr. ROHRABACHER. Well, thank you very much, Mr. Chairman.

I would remind Mr. Sherman that I have a piece of legislation that suggests that we should not be permitting more Chinese journalists to come to the United States than they permit us to have our journalists come and operate in China. So reciprocity would be, I think, one tool, especially considering that the vast majority of their so-called journalists are actually spies and people who have come here to do us harm and propagandize for their dictatorship rather than trying to find honest information to provide for the Chinese people. So I would think that would be a good way to deal with that.

We don't seem to have any reciprocity with the Chinese. I mean, didn't we give most favored nation status to China after they slaughtered the democracy movement in Tiananmen Square? What was our reciprocity there? In fact, it was just the opposite. We gave them a reward even though they had just committed an evil action. WTO was, of course, permanent most favored nation status, was granted by the Clinton administration. Let me just note again this is bipartisan in the sense that Herbert Walker Bush was the one who originally came out kissing the feet of these gangsters in Beijing and followed by Bill Clinton, all anxious to do favors for these omnipotent rulers of Beijing who rule with an iron fist.

China is, because of its size and other factors, should be considered the world's worst human rights abuser. We were told there would be some impact on that if we just simply did business with them. And I think, Mr. Sherman, before you leave, I would like to make sure I back up your point—I don't think he hears me—back up his point. The Chinese are not, as you say, outdoing us economically because of the American worker. We have given enormous economic benefits to them in terms of an open market, in terms of capital investment, in terms of turning our face away and letting them get away with the massive threat of American technology which has basically permitted them to introduce products to the market that were based on our R&D. So they don't have any R&D costs. We are picking it all up for them. No wonder they can charge less.

I think that the people of Hong Kong are our greatest ally in the fight for freedom and peace in this world because they are confronting the world's worst human rights abuser. Just as when we ignored and betrayed the people in the Tiananmen Square democracy movement, we now have a world that is less peaceful, we now have a world that is more at risk because of this vicious dictatorship that stays in power. The young people, the young activists in Hong Kong today, if they are successful, will create a better world, a more peaceful world, a world in which the Chinese and American people will deal with each other as equals and not having a President being afraid to bring up whatever issue with the leader, with his counterpart in Beijing.

I think that it is quite obvious where we could actually be doing things that would counteract or at least put ourselves to be taken seriously by the Chinese. There are things we could be doing, and especially when it comes in the economic area.

But also, look, when the Chinese Government decides that they are going to commit armed force against people who have a territorial dispute, whether it is against India, whether it is against Japan, whether it is against the Philippines, whether it is against Vietnam——

Mr. CONNOLLY. Or Crimea.

Mr. ROHRABACHER. Well, that is what I am saying. In Crimea, Putin sends a couple troops across the border into areas that want to be part of Russia and we go bananas. But China commits all of this force across the way in disputed territories, there is no price to pay. Well, we need to have a little bit more of a consistent pro-freedom policy, and if we do, like the people in Hong Kong, like the activists in Hong Kong, the people of this world will help build a better world, and we will be on their side.

Thank you very much.

Mr. CHABOT. Thank you. The gentleman's time has expired.

The gentleman from the Commonwealth of Virginia is recognized for 5 minutes.

Mr. CONNOLLY. I thank my friend, and I couldn't resist helping my friend from California because I wanted him to have an all-inclusive list.

Thank you, panel, for being here. And I want to get in two sets of questions if I can. I pray I can get it in.

One is, I would be very interested, and I am going to start with you, Dr. Richardson, because you said the problem is not that the Obama administration hasn't done good things in human rights and other areas, it has, but the problem is no policy. I would like to explore that. What ought to be our policy in Hong Kong, and what is our leverage? Let's have a realistic, not a quixotic policy.

And then secondly, the second question I want to get at with the three of you is, what is the impact on Taiwan? Taiwan is watching all of this. If there was any appetite in Taiwan, and there was, for maybe a similar model some day in the future, what is the impact on Chinese behavior vis—vis Hong Kong, do you think, on those aspirations or those political dynamics in Taiwan?

So the first question, what ought to be our policy? And what leverage do we have to try to fashion it?

Ms. RICHARDSON. Let me try to answer the first one very quickly about policy. I think one of the big problems is that 15 years ago when we were having the PNTR debate, human rights issues occupied a much larger piece of the policy pie. And as the relationship has deepened and expanded and there are dozens and hundreds of competing interests, the amount of time and attention that is given to human rights issues has shrunk.

What we have wanted to see is a much more thoughtful policy approach that recognizes human rights issues and human rights protections as fundamental to a host of different issues in the relationship. Quite like Mr. Rohrabacher's point about pro-democracy protestors in Hong Kong as allies, these are the people who are arguing for protections that are just as important for their electoral processes as they are for U.S. businesses to do what they do and succeed in that part of the world. It is about a free press and an independent judiciary and a free flow of information.

I think the fact that no more thoughtful policy has been developed such that human rights-related requests or demands can be leveled by many different actors in the U.S. relationship, that it remains almost exclusively the purview or the burden of the State Department as they sometimes view it, has made it very easy for the Chinese Government to essentially minimize and not react to the kinds of demands that are made.

There are certain practical tactics that really aren't used very well any more, the demands of releases. Even the clarification after the President's visit of the human rights-related requests that were made in advance of the visit that weren't fulfilled. Right? I mean, there are levers that aren't being pulled, but there is also the very obvious value of public rhetoric and challenging Chinese officials publicly, which is something they deeply dislike and usually will move to try to avoid. And I think making that a regular part of an interaction, whether it is Secretary Johnson or whoever runs the Pentagon or Secretary Kerry, is critical. I am going to leave the Taiwan question.

Mr. CONNOLLY. Yeah. I agree with you wholeheartedly, and I think human rights always must be a hallmark of U.S. diplomacy, and we retreat from who we are when we don't make it one. Having said that, it must also be done carefully and subtly, that question of leverage again.

Well, if I announce that I am forming Democrats for Chabot for Speaker, I guarantee you that is not helpful to Steve Chabot and in some quarters might even make him suspect, that he is so friendly with people like me. So in a more serious vein, we need to be careful that with the best of intentions we don't put a target on somebody by virtue of our blessing and imprimatur. So it has to be done with skill, is my only point.

Ms. RICHARDSON. I am all for skill, and I am all for nuance, but I also think we are not yet at a point in time—and we should be— where a host of interests across the U.S. Government recognize the Ilham Tohtis, the Puder Changs, the Gao Yus, all of these people who have gone to prison in China as allies for their interests as well and go to bat for them.

Mr. CONNOLLY. That is right.

Ms. RICHARDSON. This is not an enormous analytical leap. And this problem is getting significantly worse in the mainland, and it requires a much more robust response.

Mr. CONNOLLY. Good point.

Mr. Cheng, on Taiwan.

Mr. CHENG. Very quickly, sir, 2016 will be a crucial year, and I would predict that we are going to be looking at much worse cross-straits relations. The recent elections in Taiwan have already seen a significant growth in DPP popularity and power. This was not necessarily key to what has been going on in Hong Kong specifically, but there is no question that the people in Taiwan who are skeptical of reunification look at what has happened in Hong Kong as a very important warning.

The cross-straits relationship has been calm for the last 6 years, in no small part because President Ma Ying-jeou chose not to emphasize independence. But the prospect of a pro-independence government arising in Taipei is especially difficult to calculate because Xi Jinping himself was not within the inner circle of power when there was a previous DPP President.

So essentially you could wind up in 2016 with three sets of leaders, all of whom have very different interests, a potential DPP President possibly, but certainly more pro-independence sentiment on the island; Xi Jinping, who would be confronted with a pro-independence attitude on the island; and of course we ourselves are going to be very, very focused on our own electoral politics, and perhaps, as the ranking member noted, not necessarily paying the right amount of attention to that region as the pot begins to boil.

Mr. CONNOLLY. Thank you. And Mr. Cheng is a constituent of mine, and his brilliance is obvious.

Mr. CHABOT. Thank you. The gentleman's time has expired.

We will go on a second round, but we are going to have votes here very shortly, so if we can keep it. I will just ask one question. And my colleague and friend from Virginia has already brought it up. I was going to talk about Taiwan, so I will just bring it up very briefly because you already addressed it, Mr. Cheng, very well.

And that is, relative to Taiwan, obviously they can't have helped but observe China's thuggish behavior in Hong Kong, and I think it probably did send a message in the recent election to some degree because KMT was soundly defeated in the local elections around the country.

Now, President Ma, to his credit, had spoken out in favor of the Hong Kong protestors. And so you addressed the question really. I just really wanted to get back, as one of the cofounders of the Congressional Taiwan Caucus, what impact will this have, if any, on the public's attitude toward China and reconciliation versus independence versus maintaining the status quo, et cetera?

Mr. CHENG. As we saw this summer with the Sunflower Movement which took over the Taiwan legislature, there is a growing unease, frankly unhappiness in Taiwan toward the current status quo. There is a perception that the island is falling ever more under the sway of Beijing. And if Beijing were living up to its commitments, was truly valuing things like ''One Country, Two Systems'', that might produce one dynamic. But as we have seen in Hong Kong, what this really is saying is, from the people of Taiwan it seems, we don't trust you as a partner.

Now, the problem is that, and we saw some of this in Hong Kong, is Beijing doesn't take to that sort of skepticism very well. And the sad reality is that Taiwan's security is eroding. There have been reports from our own military about how Taiwan's ability to control the air space and sea space around the island is deteriorating. There has not been a major arms sale to Taiwan in years. The recent sales have mostly been fulfilling previous commitments dating back over a decade. Taiwan has been asking for the U.S. to allow teams to go and study the problem in Taiwan, and those requests apparently are sitting on some State Department desk for years.

By the way, this is bipartisan. It is not simply this administration. They has been sitting on those desks dating back to the previous administration. This sends a signal, unfortunately, to Taiwan that maybe you should try and cut a deal, unfortunately, with an unreliable partner.

Mr. CHABOT. And if I were a resident in Taiwan, I would be particularly concerned when they hear stories about the administration's goal to reduce our military back to pre-World War II levels at a time when the PRC has increased their military expenditures by double digits every year for the last 25 years.

That being said, I think that the U.S. should continue to maintain a very strong relationship with Taiwan, and we should be there for them. They are a role model for other countries around the world, and we shouldn't let them be bullied by the PRC.

That being said, I will yield back the balance of my time and turn to the gentleman from American Samoa.

Mr. FALEOMAVAEGA. Mr. Chairman, I have no further questions other than to again thank our distinguished panelists for their statements and their positions. And I certainly want to thank you for your leadership and your service to our committee and to our country. Yes, this will be my last subcommittee hearing, and it has been my distinct honor and privilege of having served with you and the other members of the committee, hopefully being helpful in developing a better world.

Thank you, Mr. Chairman.

Mr. CHABOT. Thank you very much.

The gentleman from Pennsylvania.

Mr. PERRY. Thank you, Mr. Chairman.

I will turn to Mr. Cheng. We spoke briefly prior to this about China and the fact that they aren't a very good neighbor. They are happy to—well, we in this country are oftentimes accused from within and without of being imperialist. They on the other hand go ahead and take the minerals and the raw materials—with a deal, they make a deal with somebody, some nation, to take the raw materials. And as you aptly put it, they don't lecture. Of course, they are not in any position to lecture, but they don't lecture. They are happy to do that. But as a world actor on the world stage, they are not a very good neighbor in the way that we would see one.

That having been said, why do you suppose there is this reluctance from this administration to take quantifiable action regarding Beijing's actions in Hong Kong—cyber crime, the physical incursions in the China Sea, et cetera. Why do you suppose there is this reluctance? And I said to you, and I just want you to recount your statement, I said to you, is it because we borrow so much money from them and we are concerned that that would jeopardize that? If you could just elaborate.

Mr. CHENG. Sir, I do not believe that the administration is reticent because of the concern over issues of debt, because, frankly, China purchases American debt more because of the situation with its own currency which is under very tight control, which is not free floating. China is not really in a position to replace the U.S. as a global reserve currency. It is buying American debt because it is probably the best and safest place to put China's surpluses short of building the world's largest mattress and stuffing all of that money underneath.

I do believe, however, that the administration has chosen to value other things more highly than in some cases our principles and in other cases our traditional strategic interests. The administration, for example, trumpeted the climate change agreement as a huge advance despite lacking in details. This dates back to 2009 when the administration made very clear that what it wanted from China more than anything else was an agreement at the Copenhagen climate talks.

So I believe that the administration is pursuing what for it is a rational choice of saying what they value, which seems to be on issues of things like climate, and on more nebulous, less concrete things from their perspective, such as human rights or American security commitments to the region, it is willing to offer those up.

Mr. PERRY. Thank you.

Moving on, I would just like to make one clarification while I have got the mike. A good friend from the other side of the aisle commented that my interest in potentially modifying the visa waiver program would be untenable because he included all of China in the discussion where I did not ever advocate for all of China, just Hong Kong specifically. I also find it very telling and interesting that he would continue with restrictions for political dissidents, meanwhile advocating for an open southern border, which he currently is, as far as I know.

That having been said, again to you, Mr. Cheng, if you can just codify very simply, what are our interests in Hong Kong, and why should Americans care? Why should Americans care? Why should we invest? What are our interests? If you can codify that pretty simply, I know that is hard to do. I have got about 1½ minutes left, which is yours.

Mr. CHENG. Sir, some of the issues at stake here, at the most materialistic end, this is a global financial hub. You create massive disruption if you have instability in one of the world's truly global financial centers. You raise questions about the American commitment to its principles when we walk away from people who want to be free.

My colleagues here have stated quite eloquently the issue of values and where they stand and how we are perceived with regards to those values and especially if we walk away from them. And, frankly, we also send the wrong message to Beijing about what is in its interests if we mislead them into thinking that they can violate agreements without consequences. At some point, if somebody keeps getting away with things, they are going to keep on doing that.

Mr. PERRY. Thank you, Mr. Chairman.

Thank you, panelists.

I yield back.

Mr. CHABOT. The gentleman's time has expired. The gentleman from Virginia is recognized.

Mr. CONNOLLY. Thank you.

First of all, Mr. Cheng, I agree with your last statement. I believe Beijing in a sense respects one thing: Power. And it is a mistake for the United States not to sell weapons to Taiwan. It is a mistake for the United States not to show, in fact, a fortified relationship with Taiwan, especially in light of the developments in Hong Kong. It is a mistake for the United States not to make it very clear, at least in diplomatic sessions with the Chinese, we care a lot about that, and it will impinge the relationship, as Dr. Richardson, I think, was suggesting in a previous answer to my question.

I do want to be fair though. I know you are from Heritage Foundation. But with respect to Mr. Perry, it is hardly limited to this administration that we pull our punches with China. I wish that were true. Since Richard Nixon went to Beijing and visited with Zhou Enlai and saw the Forbidden City and the Great Wall, every succeeding administration has made compromises that make one sad about U.S. principles and virtues and values because they are weighing various and sundry factors, and there seems to be this ethos we can't afford to make the Chinese angry. And it seems to me that that is the wrong calculus, even if it is noble in intent.

And I wonder if you might all want to comment on that because I am cochair of the Taiwan Caucus, and I feel that it is really important we not equivocate about the Taiwan Relations Act commitments to Taiwan and that Beijing is always calculating those misses. And we have now virtually given Beijing veto power over weapon system sales, as Mr. Chabot indicated, to Taiwan, and I think that is a terrible mistake. But at any rate, your views. Question of what does Beijing respect and how does that fashion or should fashion or influence U.S. policy.

Ms. CURRIE. I agree with you that this is a bipartisan problem and it largely tends to be focused in the executive branch, but not exclusively. When I worked at the State Department it was very frustrating at times to see the way in which the Department and the government as a whole, the executive branch as a whole, would curl into a self-protective ball when it came to dealing with China and choose the issues that they would raise and the way in which those issues would be raised based on the likelihood that they would provoke a negative reaction. The things that provoked the negative reaction go off the list, and the things that can be talked about safely without upsetting the Chinese stay on the list.

And our officials become conditioned over time, because the Chinese react to anything in a very hyperventilated way when they don't like what they are hearing from our officials. Whereas we are conditioned to sit and take everything that they say, no matter how offensive it is to our values, no matter how offensive it is to our interests. Our diplomats sit there and take it from the Chinese. And then when we say anything that is even mildly critical, they fly off the handle. And it is a strategic negotiating tactic that they use in the way that they deal with us.

So i think part of the problem is it goes back to the way our diplomatic corps is organized, how they are trained, what they are prepared to deal with when they go into meetings with the Chinese. They simply are not, even when they are China hands, and in some cases the China hands are the worst because they have invested all these years in learning Chinese and in making relationships with people in the Chinese Government. The last thing they want to do is screw up their career by alienating their interlocutors.

So one of the big problems is trying to get people out of this mind frame that the relationship is the most important thing about our relationship. It is not. The relationship is a means to an end. And our interests and our values are the same thing when it comes to China. These two fundamental issues lie at the heart of the problem with our lack of policy and our lack of strategic thinking about how to deal with China.

Mr. CONNOLLY. Thank you so much.

If the chairman will indulge, I would just like to give the other two panelists an opportunity to answer the same question. I thank the chair.

Ms. RICHARDSON. I will try to be very quick and just point out that in 1997 the great hope was not only that rights in political space in Hong Kong would be protected and possibly expand, but also that it might have a positive influence on the mainland. And we are here today because we are seeing the opposite. And I think if the U.S. really does believe that democracies and rights-respecting governments make better trade partners, make better strategic allies, make more reliable partners across a host of issues, there is a lot more work to be done with respect to China.

I think it is also deeply problematic. It is not just a question of people I think scaling back their expectations of diplomatic initiatives or what the Chinese Government may or may do, I think there is almost a complete absence from these discussions about what people more broadly in China want and supporting that and expressing some solidarity with people who are trying to make precisely the kind of change that I think is fundamental to the U.S. achieving its long-term policy goals. Again, it goes back to the point about seeing various activists in the mainland as key allies for lots of different interests in the U.S., not as sort of the human rights box to be checked.

Mr. CHENG. Sir, the key and fundamental difference here is that China knows what it wants. It pushes for those goals, and it pushes them with every lever at its disposal, which given a centralized authority means economic, industry, official spokespeople, media, et cetera.

We need to be consistent in our policy objectives and persistent in enunciating them. We need to apply not only the State Department and the Commerce Department and the levers of government in the executive branch and also here in the legislative branch, but also to encourage business, to encourage NGOs, to encourage media and other places to be as forthright in standing up for those American principles, not American Government principles, but American principles, as the Chinese are in standing up for theirs.

I don't fault the Chinese for standing up for what they believe in. That is their business. I do fault us for not applying all of those levers in a consistent manner persistently.

Mr. CHABOT. Thank you. The gentleman's time has expired. All time has expired. And we want to thank the panel for its testimony here this afternoon. We are being called to the floor for votes now. All members will have 5 days to supplement their remarks or submit questions.

And I want to once again thank Mr. Faleomavaega for his service to this committee, to American Samoa, and to our country. We really did mean all those nice things that we said about him.

And if there is no further business to come before the committee, we are adjourned. Thank you.

[Whereupon, at 3:44 p.m., the subcommittee was adjourned.]

APPENDIX

MATERIAL SUBMITTED FOR THE RECORD

SUBCOMMITTEE HEARING NOTICE
COMMITTEE ON FOREIGN AFFAIRS
U.S. HOUSE OF REPRESENTATIVES
WASHINGTON, DC 20515-6128

Subcommittee on Asia and the Pacific
Steve Chabot (R-OH), Chairman

November 25, 2014

TO: MEMBERS OF THE COMMITTEE ON FOREIGN AFFAIRS

You are respectfully requested to attend an OPEN hearing of the Committee on Foreign Affairs, to be held by the Subcommittee on Asia and the Pacific in Room 2172 of the Rayburn House Office Building (and available live on the Committee website at www.foreignaffairs.house.gov):

DATE: Tuesday, December 2, 2014

TIME: 2:00 p.m.

SUBJECT: Hong Kong: A Broken Promise?

WITNESSES: Mr. Dean Cheng
                   Senior Research Fellow
                   Asian Studies Center
                   The Davis Institute for National Security and Foreign Policy
                   The Heritage Foundation

                   Sophie Richardson, Ph.D.
                   China Director
                   Human Rights Watch

                   Ms. Kelley Currie
                   Senior Fellow
                   Project 2049 Institute

By Direction of the Chairman

The Committee on Foreign Affairs seeks to make its facilities accessible to persons with disabilities. If you are in need of special accommodations, please call 202/225-5021 at least four business days in advance of the event, whenever practicable. Questions with regard to special accommodations in general (including availability of Committee materials in alternative formats and assistive listening devices) may be directed to the Committee.

COMMITTEE ON FOREIGN AFFAIRS

MINUTES OF SUBCOMMITTEE ON _____ *Asia & the Pacific* _____ HEARING

Day___*Tuesday*___Date_____*2:00 p.m.*___Room_____*2172*_____

Starting Time ___*2:00 p.m.*___ Ending Time ___*3:44 p.m.*___

Recesses [____] (____to ____) (____to ____) (____to ____) (____to ____) (____to ____) (____to ____)

Presiding Member(s)
Chairman Steve Chabot (R-OH), Ranking Member Eni Faleomavaega (D-AS)

Check all of the following that apply:

Open Session ☑
Executive (closed) Session ☐
Televised ☑

Electronically Recorded (taped) ☐
Stenographic Record ☑

TITLE OF HEARING:
Hong Kong: A Broken Promise?

SUBCOMMITTEE MEMBERS PRESENT:
Rep. Scott Perry (R-PA), Rep. Ami Bera (D-CA), Rep. Brad Sherman (D-CA), Rep. Matt Salmon (R-AZ), Rep. Dana Rohrabacher (R-CA), Rep. Mo Brooks (R-AL), Rep. Gerald Connolly (D-VA)

NON-SUBCOMMITTEE MEMBERS PRESENT: *(Mark with an * if they are not members of full committee.)*

HEARING WITNESSES: Same as meeting notice attached? Yes ☑ No ☐
(If "no", please list below and include title, agency, department, or organization.)

STATEMENTS FOR THE RECORD: *(List any statements submitted for the record.)*

TIME SCHEDULED TO RECONVENE _____
or
TIME ADJOURNED ___*3:44 p.m.*___

_____
Subcommittee Staff Director

Statement for the Record
Submitted by Mr. Connolly of Virginia

When China announced in a June 2014 white paper that Hong Kong's march toward universal suffrage would come with a caveat, that candidates for Hong Kong Chief Executive must be vetted and PRC-approved, public reaction was understandably tinged with feelings of outrage and betrayal. In a region with a population of 7.2 million people, as many as 100,000 protestors took to the streets and founded a movement that continues to this day.

It is hard to ignore the plight of the Hong Kong protestors against the backdrop of force and aggression China has painted in the Asia-Pacific. Maritime disputes in the South and East China Seas have led many regional powers to conclude that China's desire to exercise more control over the region will come at the expense of its neighbors. Similarly, we can expect China's tightened grip on Hong Kong to be to the detriment of democratic institutions that contravene Communist Party ideology.

Hong Kong's degree of autonomy is firmly rooted in long-standing legal precedent and should not be subject to change by fiat. The Sino-British Joint Declaration that was signed by the People's Republic of China (PRC) and the United Kingdom in December 1984 and registered at the United Nations in June 1985 remains the binding agreement on which the "one country, two systems" model operates. Furthermore, Hong Kong's constitutional document, the Basic Law, formally enshrined Hong Kong's principles of autonomy and domestic self-governance not by independent means, but through adoption by the National People's Congress in April 1990.

The Hong Kong Special Administrative Region is, by definition, unique within China. The capitalist economic system and individual freedoms that define Hong Kong would be unrecognizable on the mainland. For this reason, assurances of continuity have always been the foundation of Hong Kong's reversion process. When the world awoke on July 1, 1997 to a new flag flying over Hong Kong, there was concern that this new era would witness the erosion of civil liberties and basic freedoms in Hong Kong. To that end, promises were made, and those promises must be kept.

If China is unable to resolve this dispute in a manner that honors past agreements, the Umbrella Movement could serve as a particularly important lesson for the renewed focus on U.S. alliance-building in the Asia-Pacific. Countries and people threatened by China's willingness to upend regional stability will consider both resistance and acquiescence. The U.S. can influence their calculus to resist China's aggression if a close relationship with the U.S. is made to be synonymous with reliability and security.

The "one country, two systems" model was originally devised by Beijing as a framework for the China-Taiwan Cross-Strait relationship. However, Taiwan, bolstered by the assurances made by the U.S. in the Taiwan Relations Act of 1979, has resisted falling into China's orbit. We must rededicate ourselves to that commitment. For its part, the House of Representatives earlier this year reiterated support for supplying Taiwan with defensive military capabilities. In April, the House passed H.R. 3470, the Taiwan Relations Act Affirmation and Naval Vessel Transfer Act of 2014, authorizing the sale of four Oliver Hazard Perry-class guided missile frigates to Taiwan.

Furthermore, Congress has on several occasions lent its support for selling Taiwan 66 F-16 C/D aircraft, most recently through the adoption of a bipartisan amendment I offered to the National Defense Authorization Act.

Honoring our commitment to Taiwan is critical to an effective U.S. presence in the Asia-Pacific, and could stand in stark contrast to China's behavior in the region, which is increasingly defined by acts similar to the betrayal of Hong Kong.

www.ingramcontent.com/pod-product-compliance
Lightning Source LLC
Chambersburg PA
CBHW081243280526
45787CB00006B/2783